Overcoming the trials of humanity
with God's guidance

The Earth says:
"All you need *is*
Love"

HS PRESS

Overcoming the trials of humanity
with God's guidance

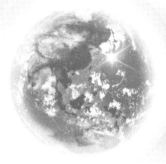

The Earth says:
"All you need *is*
Love"

EL CANTARE

Ryuho Okawa

HS PRESS

Contents

CHAPTER ONE

The Earth says:
"All you need is Love"

—The Teachings of Ame-no-Mioya-Gami
and the True World Justice—

1 My Wish Is to Spread the Teachings to Every Corner
of the World 14

2 Ame-no-Mioya-Gami, the Source of the Japanese
Civilization

In Japan, religion started 30,000 years ago when
Ame-no-Mioya-Gami descended to Earth 17

Ame-no-Mioya-Gami's teachings on how humans should
live as children of God

• The most important pillar: Live rightly 21

• The teaching for men and women: Polish your souls
as you live together 22

• The origin of Bushido: Do not live in a way that will
defile your soul.. 24

3 Why Is It Important to Believe in the Other World?

A remark from the former President of Taiwan,
Lee Teng-Hui 25

China, as a materialistic country, takes advantage of
Confucian philosophy 27

Shakyamuni Buddha taught that your thoughts and
actions will determine your afterlife 29

I want to pursue the truth as truth 33

4 The Limits of Democracy without God

The reason why I am critical of China 37

The political regime and the ruler's virtue 40

5 The Choice between Salvation and Destruction

My messages to the countries that come under China's
Belt and Road Initiative 44

The True God teaches the way to prosper with the
self-help spirit 49

CHAPTER TWO

What Is El Cantare, God of the Earth?
—A Lecture on The Laws of Faith—

1 What Is El Cantare?

Alpha and Elohim—the reincarnations of the core
consciousness of El Cantare 54

The meaning behind the name, El Cantare 61

2 The Purpose of Publishing Spiritual Messages 65

3 Overcoming Conflicts between Religions

Understanding idol worship 69

Happy Science teaches how to remove your
attachments 73

4 The Mindset Toward Prayer and Miracles

Build a strong connection with God while making
diligent efforts 74

El Cantare was the Father in Heaven who guided Jesus ... 77

Using prayer as the final step 78

5 Miracles Require Diligent Effort

The secret that keeps Happy Science going for more
than 30 years 81

Continually ask yourself if you have made progress
today 84

Keep fighting to accomplish something year after year ... 86

CHAPTER THREE

Choose Light over Darkness

—Living a Life of Service to the World—

1 The Meaning of Trials that Humankind Faces

Unexpected misfortunes teach humans lessons 90

Humble yourself before a Greater Being 92

2 An Age When a Savior Is Born

Severe trials await humankind when the world population
increases rapidly 95

Do not forget that the coronavirus infection originated
in China 97

A battle between the "communist virus" and
"faith immunity" 101

3 Japan, Be an Independent Country

Do what you can every day even during the pandemic ... 104

Raise the self-sufficiency rate in food and energy, and
create production systems 106

Japan must voice its opinions against what is wrong 108

4 The New Teachings that Will Guide the World
   to a Better Future

The world is now at a crossroads to choose between
light and darkness 110

Happy Science teachings can be summed up in four
principles 113

Gain the power to break the norms of the era 116

5 Keep Fighting through Trials and Never Let Go of
   Your Hopes

The reason why people of Uyghur, Taiwan, and
Hong Kong are counting on Happy Science 120

Be more "Rock 'n' Roll" and break through the barriers ... 123

Choose a life of service to the world 125

About the Author 131

Who Is El Cantare? 132

About Happy Science 134

Books by Ryuho Okawa 136

Music by Ryuho Okawa 147

Happy Science's English Sutra 148

Memberships 149

Contact Information 150

About HS Press 152

CHAPTER ONE

The Earth says:
"All you need is Love"

—The Teachings of Ame-no-Mioya-Gami
and the True World Justice—

Recorded in Japanese on December 14, 2021
at Saitama Super Arena in Saitama Prefecture.
English translation.

1

My Wish Is to Spread the Teachings to Every Corner of the World

Today is my 120th lecture of this year and 3,369th overall. So, one of my aspirations for next year is to reach the milestone of 3,500 lectures. I have also published over 2,900 books so far, so I aim to reach 3,000 books next year[1] [*audience applauds*]. I have been working steadily and continuously, and I am grateful to have the opportunity to do so. People do not attain enlightenment so easily [*audience laughs*], and the Laws I teach do not spread easily, either. Although I have been publishing as many as 2,900 books, if they were physically stacked in a room, I am sure it may feel intimidating to read them all. Regardless, I do not know which book will reach people's hearts nor do I know which book will appropriately guide them. People in different countries take an interest in my books on completely different topics. So, I will continue to work and make efforts ceaselessly [*audience applauds*]. Thank you very much.

Earlier on this stage, our performer sang a song that I wrote to promote our next film, which has some elements of Japanese Shinto[2]. I, myself, have chosen Japan [as my birthplace] in this lifetime and I am speaking in Japanese now, but my heart goes far beyond this country. It is my sincere wish to spread the teachings to every corner of the world.

This lecture is broadcast live via satellite to 3,500 locations worldwide and will also be repeatedly aired on national television stations in India and Nepal. So, a greater number of people—far more than in Japan— will listen to my lecture. Considering this audience, I understand that I should be speaking in English or Hindi, but I entrust it to the translators, although I do not know how well the translation will be. I hear that this lecture is kindly going to be aired a multitude of times for those who may have missed it, so I hope people will understand my message on a deeper level as they listen to it repeatedly.

In Japan, local television stations in five or six prefectures usually air the lectures I give for the "Celebration of the Lord's Descent" and the "El Cantare Celebration," oftentimes by several months' delay. If we add the number of viewers in the areas surrounding those prefectures, a considerable number of people have watched my lectures. So, even though I am speaking to my audience sitting in front of me today, this lecture will continue to be shown in various other places until the end of March next year. For that reason, I believe I must not only talk about the current issues but also mention general or universal topics.

2

Ame-no-Mioya-Gami, the Source of the Japanese Civilization

In Japan, religion started 30,000 years ago when Ame-no-Mioya-Gami descended to Earth

My audience has already heard the name Ame-no-Mioya-Gami (Japanese Father God) several times today[3]. However, I believe many people are unfamiliar with this name, including those who believe in Japanese Shinto. Shinto is a religion indigenous to Japan that has shrines with *torii* gates (gateway entrances). Its believers themselves think that its history can only be traced back to no more than 3,000 years, about 2,700 years. Perhaps this cannot be helped because there is little record of it. However, starting around 2015, I have been continuing to reveal that the Japanese civilization began about 30,000 years ago when Ame-no-Mioya-Gami traveled from the universe and descended to a place near Mt. Fuji. I have spoken about this in several books I published in the past.

Today, too, we could see Mt. Fuji in the distance from this location, Saitama Prefecture, despite the bad weather. Historically, before Ame-no-Mioya-Gami arrived, there was a second Mt. Fuji near it. It was smaller and similar to the shape of Mt. Fuji. When Ame-no-Mioya-Gami arrived from the Andromeda Galaxy 30,000 years ago on a spaceship called Ame-no-Torifune, the craft landed on this second smaller version of Mt. Fuji, crushing the mountain into a wide hill by the sheer weight of His spaceship. Some of the crafts that came together with the spaceship are still buried at the foot of Mt. Fuji which is located within Shizuoka Prefecture. So I would like to reveal more details about this at a later time.

My point here is that contrary to common belief, the Japanese religious culture originated not 3,000 years ago, but 10 times earlier—30,000 years ago. Today, I would like to introduce some of the original teachings that created the religious culture in Japan. But this is not to say that this religion was only believed in Japan. The Japanese archipelago is currently made up of small islands surrounded by the sea, but it was different 30,000 years ago; both the southern and northern parts were connected to the Eurasian Continent at the time. So, the people, as well as animals, were able to travel freely between there and Japan. Naturally, the teachings of Ame-no-Mioya-Gami 30,000 years ago also spread across the Eurasian Continent in one form or another. First, I would like you to know this fact as it may take some time before I can reveal more details of those times.

It is generally believed that Japan became civilized when people from the continent migrated to the small islands of Japan and spread their culture. Others say the Japanese civilization was formed after people from the south canoed up north from island to island to settle in Japan. However, what I have revealed is completely different.

Although the Japanese chronicles *Kojiki* and *Nihon Shoki* mention nothing about Ame-no-Mioya-Gami, His name can be found in an older history book called, *Hotsuma-Tsutae*. *Kojiki* and *Nihon Shoki* were written in the early eighth century, whereas *Hotsuma-Tsutae*, which has a description of Ame-no-Mioya-Gami, was presumably written at least as early as around the fourth century, or even earlier. Most of its content was probably established by the beginning of the second century. This means that

Ame-no-Mioya-Gami's teachings were compiled at around the same time as when the Christian Bible was written. Jesus was born in 4 B.C. and died around 30 A.D. The Jews then perished during the Siege of Masada around 70 A.D. After that, Jesus' teachings were passed down orally until they were finally compiled into the Bible from around the end of the first century to the beginning of the second century. This is what is believed in Christianity. Around the same time, the record of Ame-no-Mioya-Gami's teachings had already existed in Japan, so we can assume His legends had already been handed down before that.

He left a great number of teachings, so I will only describe them briefly. Some of what He taught were Japanese-oriented, but its contents were universal enough to be adapted to cultures other than Japan. I would like to introduce some of them today and extend into the topic of, "The Earth says: 'All you need is Love.'"

As for the appearance of Ame-no-Mioya-Gami, it would be better for you to see images of Him rather than hearing me describe Him in words. It was said that 30,000 years ago when His spaceship landed on the foot of Mt. Fuji, about 200,000 people came along, who then became the original ancestors of the Japanese people today. This suggests that quite a number of ships—more than hundreds—had come. I think I will be able to talk about it in more detail at a later time. Ame-no-Mioya-Gami was a large figure, so apparently, He could not adapt to life on Earth so easily and had a hard time acclimatizing Himself. We can get a glimpse of Ame-no-Mioya-Gami's core teachings from the traditional ideas of Japan that have been passed down for generations to this day.

Ame-no-Mioya-Gami's teachings on how humans should live as children of God

•The most important pillar: Live rightly

One of His teachings that I must mention first is the following: "*Humans must live as children of God or Buddha. To do so, they must live rightly.*" This was an important pillar. It means humans are not here only to "survive" in this world. There is more that humans should do other than acquire food and live on earth. He taught people to live rightly. Therefore, self-exploration as a human being was to think about what it means to live rightly.

·The teaching for men and women: Polish your souls as you live together

He gave different teachings to men and women. To men, He taught them to be masculine, which is a teaching that can also be applied to men today. What does it mean to be masculine? This is what He taught: "*Don't live dishonestly and solely think about your own selfish desire or benefit. Instead, dedicate your life to living for the sake of many people. Live honorably without lying or deceiving others.*" Do men of today live up to this? How many men can say, "That is how I live"? Perhaps it is an overstatement to say that 10 percent of men can say it; there is probably less.

Then, what did He teach women? He was generally kind to women, but also strict in some respects. He said, "*Women play a crucial role in allowing humankind to continuously undergo soul training on earth. The world would have been much simpler if humans were all male or all female, but in reality, both men and women were created. As a result, life in this world has become much more complicated requiring everyone to overcome a more variety of challenges. Sustaining families and producing offspring have also become difficult issues. So, men and women must strive to solve these complicated challenges and work together to create an ideal nation."*

I believe He also guided women to be stronghearted. It may be rare to see stronghearted women today, but back then, they were expected to stand their ground and firmly tell off their children if they were lazy, delinquent, or going astray. They were also expected to be stern toward their husbands and straighten them out if they did not work and stayed idle at home. Ame-no-Mioya-Gami believed that it was a woman's job to make a man a real man. Women in those times were quite strong, so if men were slow and weak, women would take the lead and fight at the forefront. In all ages, there are smart women as well as quick-witted women. That is why Ame-no-Mioya-Gami taught that men and women must learn from their differences and polish their souls together as they live with one another.

•The origin of Bushido: Do not live in a way that will defile your soul

One of the religious teachings that Ame-no-Mioya-Gami taught was the importance of manners and obedience. He clearly told people, "*Never think that the things on this earth are all and everything.*" He always taught them, "*The real world is heaven that exists in the Spirit World, a place you will go to after you leave this physical world. Life on earth is limited. So, do not live in a way that will make you regret your life after returning to the other world.*" This meant that you must not live in a way that will make you feel ashamed of yourself.

Live nobly as a human being. Do not live in a way that would make you feel embarrassed of yourself if others were to see you. Life on earth is short, so in that short amount of time, do not fall to corruption or do anything that will defile your soul. These are His teachings. I believe they are the origin of Bushido, or the Samurai spirit.

3

Why Is It Important to Believe in the Other World?

A remark from the former President of Taiwan, Lee Teng-Hui

In 2019, I went to Taiwan to give a lecture. The day after the lecture, I visited Tamsui district, the hometown of the former President of Taiwan, Lee Teng-Hui. I once read a very interesting passage in one of his books. Mr. Lee Teng-Hui clearly stated that the Japanese philosophy was far superior to the Chinese Confucian philosophy. I had never read such a remark anywhere else; his book was the first.

One of the main books of Confucian philosophy is *The Analects*, but there is nothing written about the other world or the afterlife. When Confucius was asked about it, he replied, "I still don't understand the meaning of living life. How could I know about the world after death when I still don't know the meaning of this life?"

Confucius answered along the lines of this as written in *The Analects*. Referring to this passage, Mr. Lee Teng-Hui wrote, "Japan has Bushido, the Samurai spirit. At least, there is a book called *Hagakure* (literally, "Hidden Leaves") written by Jocho Yamamoto in the Edo Period (the 18th century) that said Bushido, or the way of the samurai, is found in death."

Of course, death itself is not our aim. Our lifespan in this world is very short. We spend a considerable amount of time in the Spirit World and only spend some decades in this world when we are born. Based on this truth, it is important to constantly be aware that you will die one day and think about what you can leave behind.

Are you making the right decisions?

Are you living rightly?

Are you living a deceitful life?

Are you deluding someone else's life?

Are you doing any wrong?

Are you doing what is right?

Are you being kind to others?

Are you comforting the people who are suffering?

By asking yourself these questions every day, and keeping in mind that you will eventually pass away, it is imperative to awaken to the meaning of life in this world, and the true meaning of "Live each day as if it were your last." This is the Japanese Bushido spirit. So, Mr. Lee Teng-Hui wrote that Japanese people embodied a philosophy that surpassed that of Confucius because they lived their lives knowing that they would die one day and asking themselves what legacy they could leave behind.

China, as a materialistic country, takes advantage of Confucian philosophy

Mr. Lee Teng-Hui's comment may have been an overpraise. I believe not many people have gained a deep insight into the Bushido spirit as he had written in his book. China has now established many Confucius Institutes around the world. The Confucian philosophy is convenient for them because it does not mention the Spirit World. It is said that Confucius did not talk about spirits, souls, ghosts in the afterlife, or the Spirit World. This makes a good match with the current China's materialistic ideology. Since the Confucian philosophy only focuses on the matters of this physical world, all China needs to do is to make science have supremacy above everything else and aim to gain material abundance.

Indeed, matters of this world are vital; it is important for science and technology to make advancements and for people to have food, clothing, and housing to live in this world. Those are necessities for physical human life, and we cannot neglect the importance of them. However, it is a mistake to believe that material things are all that matters in life.

Some countries are established based on atheistic or materialistic ideologies. It is of course important for them to strive to improve areas they are still developing. However, if materialistic countries move in the direction of advocating that only this world exists, then they are mistaken. This is not only true with China but also with Europe and the United States. In the U.S., some people go to church on Sundays but may not be mindful of the Spirit World or religious values during working hours on weekdays. They only focus on tasks in front of them and work just to make money. Unfortunately, people's faith has become shallow in content worldwide where their main focus has become gaining material abundance and making financial gain. This trend is prevailing everywhere, which is very disappointing.

This is a very small first step, but humans must know that they are not just a physical body. If they believe that they are nothing more than a physical body, their foundations are misplaced. If this starting point is mistaken, education will also be misdirected. People will pursue education for the purpose of obtaining an easier life and seeking tangible results becomes their only objective. Consequently, they will come to understand that success is to attain a higher position of power that other people will admire or to obtain things such as land, buildings, and financial resources. There are an increasing number of people who think like this.

Shakyamuni Buddha taught that your thoughts and actions will determine your afterlife

There are issues with religious nations as well. Even though certain countries believe in the idea of reincarnation, they explain it as follows: People who are wealthy or in privileged positions, such as a royal family or priest class, were born into them because they did good deeds in their past lives. India has many beliefs of this kind. This belief is deeply rooted in some countries, but when Shakyamuni Buddha descended to India about 2,500 years ago, he taught differently.

Shakyamuni Buddha was born into Kshatriya or the class of kings and warriors. In India's caste system, the top of the class hierarchy is Brahmin, the priest class. This class is the highest because they are the closest to the gods. Then there is Kshatriya or the ruler class, followed by the merchant class called Vaishya, then the Shudra, which is the slave class. These are the four main classes in the caste system. Below the main classes are the outcastes, and the people in this group are called "untouchables." So, even if people believe in the idea of reincarnation, it is often used as an excuse to legitimize their current circumstances.

For instance, they explain that you were born into a lower caste because you committed a crime in your past life, or you were born into a higher class because you did virtuous deeds in your past life. However, Shakyamuni Buddha's teachings were different.

People do not become Brahmins by birth
But by their actions.
Your actions determine who you are.
If your actions are those of Brahmins,
Then you are a Brahmin, indeed.
Put simply, if you are living as a religious person,
You are a Brahmin.
Even if you are born a Brahmin,
If you take up a sword to fight in a battle,
Then you are a Kshatriya;
And if you engage in commerce,
You are a Vaishya;
If your actions are indecent,
It means you are no different from a Shudra.
People shall be judged only through their actions.

This is what Shakyamuni Buddha taught. To add to his teachings, actions alone are not sufficient. Your thoughts will also matter. What you think in your mind will be reflected directly in your actions, so the thoughts and the corresponding actions will determine the kind of person you are.

Although India is a great religious country, it is unfortunate that the caste system still exists. Many believe that those with high status must have been virtuous in their past lives and in this lifetime. The truth is that even if people are in higher ranks or in wealthy classes, many end up in hell after death. In this world, there are many kings, cabinet ministers, high government officials, and presidents of large companies, but not all of them will go to heaven; some unfortunately fall into the pits of hell. The same goes for scholars. I want to believe that most scholars are not involved in criminal activity. However, there was a recent scandal of large tax evasion at a Japanese university with the largest enrollment, so I am growing skeptical of scholars, too. I am concerned that university staffs have downgraded and are not doing the job they should be doing, although I do not want to take it in such a negative way.

In truth, your corporate title or appearance does not determine who you are. Rather, your thoughts and actions determine your life, and they show your true value as a human being. How you live in this lifetime will determine where you will go in the afterlife, and determine the circumstances in which you will be born in your next life. This is what Shakyamuni Buddha taught.

I want to pursue the truth as truth

Even after studying difficult Indian philosophies, many scholars end up comprehending Shakyamuni Buddha's teachings from a materialistic point of view. This way of understanding is the mainstream among Japanese Buddhist scholars. I truly pity them. The cause is partially due to the misguided post-war education. After Japan was defeated in World War II, Japanese Shinto collapsed. The Shinto world in heaven, Takamagahara, also collapsed in the Spirit World to the point where it needs much repairing. This means the Japanese people's faith in Shinto gods has weakened, and as a result, their belief in the Spirit World also weakened. That is why even Buddhist scholars now think that it is more fashionable to understand Buddhism in a materialistic way.

The same goes for philosophers. If you read the original teachings of Socrates and Plato in modern language, it is apparent that they believed in spirits and souls, the other world, and also reincarnation. This is an undeniable fact; it is written clearly in their works. They had experienced spiritual phenomena, just as I do now. Now that over 2,000 years have passed since their time, many philosophers have become just like mathematicians; they use formulas and symbols to explain philosophy. Unfortunately, the current philosophy does not contain any teachings and has become useless. The work that these so-called scholars are producing is unworthy of their salaries. Their minds have become like machines, and this is indeed a shame.

Mathematics and physics are certainly useful as practical subjects. They are useful, for example, when making advanced vehicles, buildings, and spacecraft. So, I understand that those who majored in humanities should not deny the importance of mathematics and physics. Indeed, useful things should be developed and become more useful. Even so, I would like to clearly state that they must not forget the most important thing that lies at the basis of these studies. These scholars must learn to discipline themselves by refraining from evaluating topics that are beyond their specialization. To be humble enough to say, "I do not know," to things they do not fully understand is of great importance. The time may come when they will have to study matters beyond their specialty as death will eventually approach them.

If it turned out that the Spirit World does not exist, and humans being born on earth and returning to the other world after death was a lie, then it would mean that the 2,900 or more books I have written so far (at the time of the lecture) are all lies. Do I look like a liar? If you say that I do, please make your way to hell [*audience laughs*]. [*Looking around the audience.*] No one seems to see me as a liar. I dislike cheating even for a penny. I detest lies. I detest deceiving people. I dislike it. I loathe dishonest people. I do not like people who go around cheating the world.

I dislike fraud. I do not like fakes. That is why I pursue seeking what is real as real, and truth as truth.

I may not be 100 percent right all the time. There may be errors in my interpretation or what I deem to be fact regarding spiritual matters as it is sometimes difficult to confirm. However, I have no intention of deceiving people, misleading them, misguiding them, or making them miserable. I do not wish for the happiness of only myself or only for our group. I have no such intentions.

4

The Limits of Democracy without God

The reason why I am critical of China

I am aware that I speak critically about China, which has become a large materialistic nation. My heart breaks as I say things about a country that I know would make them feel unpleasant. It is not my desire to be critical. China alone has a population of 1.4 billion people and many more if we include ethnic Chinese who are living overseas. There are perhaps close to two billion Chinese people in total and many more others who are under the influence of China's materialistic values. It is against my will to let a great number of people live in the wrong way. That is why I am speaking my thoughts, even if I were to be regarded as an enemy.

Mao Zedong is considered the founding father of China, although it may not be for much longer. One hundred years ago, he established the Chinese Communist Party. He has been considered the founder of the People's Republic of China for about 70 years. With a lot of embroidered stories, he is regarded as a remarkable person. However, despite being a communist, he did not study Marx's books. This may be difficult to translate (for the simultaneous interpreters in the venue that day), but he only read a book called *Zizhi Tongjian* which was written by a Chinese historian named Sima Guang. This was the only book he read repeatedly in those days when he fled from cave to cave. When the Japanese army entered China and was fighting Chiang Kai-shek's army, Mao Zedong's Red Army retreated inland toward the area that used to be the ancient kingdom of Shu in *The Records of the Three Kingdoms*. As he fled into the recesses of the mountains and into the caves, he did not read any of Marx's books. He read *Zizhi Tongjian*, which was a book on governance that describes, in the history of more than a thousand years, how China governed its people. He repeatedly read this book and barely any foreign ones. So, he is a fake and not a true communist.

Communism includes the teachings of the Old Testament because Marx was Jewish himself. The Old Testament, which is compiled together with the New Testament, is essential to understanding the New Testament.

So even today, when Christians read the Bible, they also read the Old Testament; it contains Jewish teachings and is part of their holy scripture. So, Marx's ideology also contains the teachings of the Old Testament. It contains the concept of the millennial kingdom, a view of how a kingdom should be established. Nevertheless, this idea was not in Mao Zedong's mind because he only studied Chinese history.

Then, what is Chinese history? Sometimes, China says their nation has 4,000 years of history and at other times 5,000 years, but unfortunately during all those years, they have never once experienced democracy. So, democracy cannot be studied by reading Chinese history books alone. China has always been either unified under an autocratic dictatorship or divided into smaller kingdoms and in conflict with each other. When smaller kingdoms were in conflict, an autocrat rose to unify the country, but a revolution followed and the country was split again, only to spark another war. This cycle has occurred repetitively in their history. As a result, Chinese history books only teach how to unify the country using military force, which China regards highly. However, this idea is wrong.

The political regime and the ruler's virtue

Historically, as mentioned earlier, the teachings of Ame-no-Mioya-Gami flowed into the Chinese continent as well. In China, three generations of virtuous emperors named Yao, Shun, and Yu governed the country under "virtuocracy" during their rule. Their governance had the same spiritual Light that later flowed into Japanese Shinto, but it only lasted while those three emperors were in power.

Virtuocracy can surpass democracy at its height when a great leader is leading the country. And when democracy is at its height, it can be as good as virtuocracy. For example, when a country is governed by someone like the former U.S. President Abraham Lincoln, the name of the political system no longer matters—be it virtuocracy or democracy. Democracy and virtuocracy mean almost the same when a virtuous leader governs his or her country. So, I have no intention of judging good and evil by looking at the political system only.

Currently, U.S. President Biden is raising international tension by expressing that there is an ongoing conflict between democratic and autocratic countries. He became president by dismissing Trump's policy as a divisive approach and calling for cooperation and peace instead. But in reality, since Biden became the president, the division between countries is getting worse, and it seems to me that a world war crisis is drawing near. The U.S. has now made Russia their enemy, unlike the time during Mr. Trump's presidency. China is also now their enemy. Worsening the issues at hand, Iran is now their enemy as well, and other Islamic countries will probably end up following this trend. It is highly likely that Southeast Asian countries will also be drawn into conflict as various skirmishes are now occurring in several countries. I believe all of them were triggered by President Biden's lack of strategic insight.

No political system is perfect on earth. Even so, we must always consider the better direction for all of us to head in. Democracy is good in the sense that it can remove evil. Leaders who oppress or massacre the citizens can be voted out. This is a strength of democracy. However, that alone does not make it the best.

To run a U.S. presidential election, it costs about ¥20 billion ($140 million) for advertisement alone. Usually, people do not have this much money. An average person would not want to spend that much on advertising funds, only to be the president for four years. This is not possible in Japan as well. Comparatively, in China, if you assume a high political position, you can easily earn billions of yen because politicians collude with companies. In fact, you will find flaws in every country's political systems if you observe them closely.

An important point that must be made about democratic countries is that "democracy without God" is wrong. The correct democracy is when people, who can reflect on themselves as children of God and wish to create an ideal world as children of God, participate in politics.

Then, what would be the case for a military regime? Is it an awful system? A military regime can rise when there is a revolution, but such a regime must not persist for too long. Prolonging it will undoubtedly lead to corruption. What is necessary is virtue. Politicians must earnestly explore what virtue is and gain it. Then, what is virtue? This is a difficult path of discipline.

There is always a reason for a revolution to occur, and it is often triggered when many people are leading an excessively difficult life and are suffering. A revolution is fought to liberate people and to make their lives better.

The liberation of people and the foundation of freedom must be the true goals of a revolution.

5

The Choice between
Salvation and Destruction

My messages to the countries that come under
China's Belt and Road Initiative

Some politicians use armed forces and cling to power once they seize it. They create an upper class and begin to oppress the rest by exploiting them. Such politicians may call themselves communists, but in fact, they have no right to do so.

Recently, even Japan's public broadcasting corporation NHK changed its policy and has been reporting China's domestic affairs, perhaps out of guilty conscience. For example, NHK reported that 600 million Chinese people, out of 1.4 billion, are in the poor class and live on a monthly income of less than ¥18,000 ($120). This monthly income is the same amount as what the Japanese people earned and lived with back in the early 1960s. I think it was around then when the monthly income was that small in Japan. This means many Chinese people are still living lives in a way that Japanese people back in the 1960s did; their standard of living is the same as what the Japanese people had over 50 years ago. Six hundred million out of 1.4 billion is a little over 40 percent. This many people are in the poor class in China. This is what NHK reported.

Now that it started reporting on such news, I believe slightly more of the NHK employees will be able to return to heaven after this life. I was afraid that they were at risk of falling to hell if they had continued to keep their stance, but it seems they have slightly corrected their views.

Indeed, China is going against the ideal of communism. Communism is supposed to eliminate disparity. Its goal is to make people equal by taking the earnings from the capitalist class and redistributing them to the lower class to realize social equality. That should be the goal of communism. Communists should be calling for all proletariat, or the working class, to unite and be active in politics. In China, the situation is completely different. The 600 million people in China today do not have any means to become wealthy.

Meanwhile, the leaders of Beijing are currently promoting the Belt and Road Initiative to other countries. As part of this project, China is building highways in other countries and lending them money to build ports, airports, and apartment buildings. However, when the loans of the debtor countries turn out to be uncollectible, China forces them to sign a 99-year lease for their properties. China is doing exactly the same thing as what Europe did to Asian countries in the past. Many Asian countries are falling into China's trap.

China funded the development of a deep seaport in Sri Lanka. China's real intention was to renovate it as a port for their own warships. Now, Sri Lanka cannot pay the money back to China, so China will eventually seize the port. Also, many Chinese military forces are gathering near Nepal, Bhutan, and along the Indian border as well. China will invade these countries sooner or later. Vietnam is resisting, but they, too, are about to give in to the temptation of money. Many countries are succumbing to China's temptation.

But this is what I would like to say to these countries: You must not sell your souls for money.

You must not sell your souls for what is wrong!

People of Nepal,

I believe you will listen to my lecture on television.

Do not sell your country.

The same goes for Sri Lanka and India.

Please be cautious.

And Pakistan,

I know you are in conflict with India,

But as an Islamic nation,

Why do you not help your fellow Muslims

Who are suffering in concentration camps

In the Uyghur region?

What about other Islamic nations?

What about Iran!?

You have made a 25-year oil investment deal

With China.

I understand that you had to

In order to survive.

You are suffering from rising inflation,

And your people are struggling to make a living.

If you do nothing, there will be a revolution;

That is probably why you want China to buy your oil.

When countries around the world

Are making agreements to stop CO_2 emissions,

You agreed to a 25-year deal with China.

However, this will only lead you to destruction.

I also tell other religious countries,

Please check

Whether you are truly leading your own countries

In the right direction.

I say to Iran,

Do not rush to make nuclear weapons.

If you do,

You will end up facing the same destiny as Iraq.

This will happen not too far into the future.

So please stop.

If Israel and Iran both possess nuclear weapons,

Israel will be the one to survive.

Iran will disappear.

So, listen to my words and think twice.

Westernize your nation.

Democratize your nation.

That is the way for your country to survive!

The True God teaches the way to prosper with the self-help spirit

Countries are either religious or non-religious

And this is an issue we face.

But even people in a religious nation

Could end up destroying their own country.

Therefore, you must govern your countries

So that every citizen can make progress

And be respected.

I have a good understanding of Buddhism,

Japanese Shinto, the religions of India,

Christianity, and Judaism.

I understand Islam as well.

But Islamic fundamentalism must change!

If you do not change it,

You will head straight into the wrong path.

So, you must make changes!

Change your future!

This is the only way you can survive.

Soon, there will come an end

To the age in which fuel supply brings prosperity.

Now is the time for you to develop your country

By having every citizen create their own work.

You must choose this path.

I want to tell the same to the people of Africa.

Islam is spreading in your countries.

But it is only spreading in the poor nations.

A political system that is very similar to communism

Is spreading in these nations.

However, the True God is teaching you

The way to prosper with the self-help spirit.

Do not take my words lightly!

There is still so much I want to teach you.

To all of you listening to my lecture,

In over 164 countries[4] [where Happy Science

members reside],

Please share my words with the people around you.

Humankind can still be saved!

But if you neglect my words,

The human population may be reduced to half.

I hope to avoid stating this as the reality

Within the next 10 years.

So please believe in my words and follow me!

Please convey my words!

Thank you very much.

EDITOR'S NOTES

1 The 3,000th book, *The Road to Cultivate Yourself* (New York: IRH Press, 2022), was published in May 2022.

2 Before the lecture, there was a live performance of "There Goes A Patriot Girl," the theme song for the movie, *The Cherry Bushido* (Executive Producer and Original Story by Ryuho Okawa).

3 The music video of "The Descent of Ame-no-Mioya-Gami" was played before the lecture as a dedication song.

4 Happy Science now has members in 171 countries across the world (as of August 2024).

CHAPTER TWO

What Is El Cantare, God of the Earth?

—A Lecture on *The Laws of Faith*—

Lecture given to members.
Recorded in Japanese on January 7, 2018
at Tokyo Shoshinkan of Happy Science in Tokyo.
English translation.

1

What Is El Cantare?

Alpha and Elohim—the reincarnations of the core consciousness of El Cantare

Today, I will give a lecture on my book, *The Laws of Faith* (New York: IRH Press, 2018), which is the most important book of this year (2018). It consists of six different lectures that I have given in the past. As I reread it, I have found that it covers a variety of topics. So if those new to Happy Science read the book only once, they may find it difficult to understand everything in the book, compared to those who have been following us for a long time. Even for those who have been studying Buddha's Truth, it is my hope that you will not just skim through this book only once. Instead, if there are areas within the book you feel the need to deepen your understanding of, please repeatedly read those sections. I am certain you will be able to learn something new every time you read it.

Before this lecture, I was listening to the CD recording of my lecture at Tokyo Dome, "The Choice of Humankind," while reading its text, which is compiled in *The Laws of Faith* as Chapter 6. My impressions of the CD and the book were very different, but I suppose it cannot be helped because their format is different. The vibration you feel when listening to my actual voice is quite different from what you can feel through written words. I assume the impression you get from watching the lecture on DVD is different from listening to it on CD, too. The vibration will be stronger on DVD than on CD, and it will be even more powerful if you are in the main hall listening to my lecture live. However, the power significantly drops when it is transcribed into text, so you cannot savor the power or the spiritual vibration imbued in my words by skimming through it. You can only feel it by reading the book thoroughly and with care.

We released the six-volume CD set and the six-volume DVD set for *The Laws of Faith*. I hope you will consider your family budget and receive them to listen to or watch them again and again. If you cannot afford it, you can just purchase the book and ask those who have the DVD or CD set to lend it to you after they have studied it sufficiently. You may borrow and share it with other people, but please refrain from copying or handing it out for free. I understand that each person is living in a different situation, so please do what is best according to your available means.

My lecture CDs are often listened to by local branch managers of Happy Science while driving to save time because they have many other things to study as well. It would be dangerous if they watched a DVD while driving, so my lecture CDs are inevitable. That is one reason why we keep releasing CDs. Nevertheless, just because people are listening to my lectures on CD does not mean that they will not get into an accident while driving, especially when it comes to the part I am exclaiming; it could startle the driver and the car could crash into something. People need to be careful, especially during the New Year holidays. If they get too absorbed in my lecture, they might lose their sense of direction while driving.

Years ago, I left my house by car to give a New Year's lecture at our General Headquarters, which was located in the Kioicho Building in Tokyo at the time. On the way there, I saw two cars going up in flames on the highway. This made me realize that people often drive carelessly during the holiday season from being in a festive mood. It left me feeling a little disturbed. Our car drove past the overturned cars that were giving off smoke. I remember feeling a little unsettled about giving the New Year lecture after seeing such a scene. In this way, people can be a bit careless at certain times of the year.

At another time, when I went to our headquarters to give the first lecture of the year, our car was hit from the side when we made a turn under the highway bridge. Back then, I used to wear a *haori* and a *hakama* (a Japanese formal wear worn at ceremonies) to give a New Year's lecture, though I do not wear them anymore as I cannot move so easily in traditional Japanese clothing and footwear. When the driver who hit our car saw me wearing such clothing, he got so scared that he repeatedly apologized to us. I could have complained to him, but since it would be embarrassing for a religious leader to complain about a mere damaged car, I kept my silence. I thought I should not disturb my mind before the New Year lecture and left my driver to deal with the aftermath of the accident.

New Year seems to be the time of the year when people are not as alert as they usually are, perhaps due to drinking too much or taking a long vacation. So, problems often occur around this time of the year. So in today's New Year's lecture, I would like to start by talking about a topic that will not overly excite you or make you feel "drunk." Then gradually, I will move on to the topics that need to be discussed for this year.

You may think that nothing bad will happen to you as long as you have faith, but other people around you could still cause you trouble. So you need to be cautious toward anything that any normal person would. Going back to the earlier episode of when we were hit upon making a turn, we were not violating any traffic rules; the other car just drove straight into us and dented our car. Since our car was heavier, all passengers were safe, but the car had to go.

After the accident, we became extra cautious and bought an even sturdier car. But the door was very heavy to open, and because of it, we ended up selling it shortly afterward. My secretaries had chosen the car saying that we would survive even if we were hit by a dump truck. However, it was too big, stood out too much, and it was difficult to turn corners. We thought the car was too big to drive in Tokyo, so we let it go. I was told that people in the United States drive big cars like that; it was one of those cars that make slow turns at corners. In Japan, only the *yakuza* boss would ride such a car. No one else would drive them. Anyhow, some things are not easy.

Going back to today's topic, as I reread *The Laws of Faith*, I was concerned that I might sound arrogant in some parts of the book to those who are nonreligious or to non-members of Happy Science. My wife asked me, out of concern, not to speak in a way that might provoke criticism. I usually do not speak in a haughty way, but when I give a lecture at a large venue, I tend to get fired up and sometimes say bold things. Long-term members of Happy Science would probably understand my tendency, but those who attend my lecture for the first time might feel offended. So I hope our members would kindly explain to them the true meaning behind my words.

In truth, I do not like to speak so highly of myself, so I usually do not speak in such a way. But people around me tell me that this is why some people fail to establish their faith in me, so I should be more direct and tell people to believe in me. However, I feel uncomfortable in doing so and would hope that people outside of Happy Science would say it on my behalf, but no one seems to. The issue is that even when my disciples, including our executives, preach about the importance of having faith, they tend to talk in a way that gathers "faith" in themselves. I can understand why they do so. They probably find it difficult to carry out the local branch activities unless the branch managers talk about having faith in them. Our staff from headquarters are also prone to talk highly of themselves when they visit local branches or temples and often forget to mention me in their talks. They may think that this is something our members should already know; therefore, they do not feel the need to mention it. That is why in today's lecture, I will talk a little about myself.

The Laws of Faith not only talks about El Cantare's soul siblings but also about the age when the core consciousness of El Cantare was born on earth under the name "Alpha" about 330 million years ago. You can learn more about this in the Happy Science animation movie, *The Laws of the Universe - Part I*, which is scheduled to be released in the fall of this year (2018). It is a sequel to the movie *The Laws of the Universe - Part 0*[1]. The movie describes various matters that have never been revealed and facts I have not yet spoken at length about in my lectures. I made this movie to create an eye-opening perspective for the world, especially Hollywood, so please look forward to watching it.

The Laws of the Universe - Part I depicts the age of Alpha, while the next sequel *Part II*[1] will depict the age of Elohim. These animated movies will help you further understand the book, *The Laws of Faith*. If you watch them carefully, you will be able to grasp an understanding of what the landscape was like and what the people looked like back then.

The meaning behind the name, El Cantare

Now, I am mainly using the name, El Cantare. The word "El" was originally often used to mean God and Light. Currently, in Spanish and Italian, I think "El" is simply the equivalent of "the" in English, but it initially meant God and Light. "Cantare" is originally a Latin word which is a language that is no longer used today. It is the origin of the Italian word "cantata," which I believe is related to the term, "to sing."

Latin was widely used in Europe; it was already in use around the beginning of the Christian era and remained the common language up until the medieval period. If you spoke Latin, it automatically became proof that you were among the intelligentsia. Many Church clerics were able to read the Bible in Latin and speak Latin. Even now, exorcisms are conducted using the Latin Bible. I would be impressed if the devils could understand the language. If they could, it can be assumed that they were once clerics in their past lives before falling to hell and becoming devils. Typically, those who were born outside the country would not be able to understand it.

In Latin, "cantare" means "to possess enchanting powers." Thus, if we trace back to the original meaning of El Cantare, it means something like "God possesses enchanting powers." This is what it means in terms of etymology. So what kind of enchanting powers does God have? God has the power of love or the power of mercy that embraces humankind, and also the mystical power and the power of miracles. They are powers of salvation. There are various forms of enchanting powers, but the ones that El Cantare has are mystical powers that work like magic. I have been explaining the meaning of El Cantare in various ways, such as "Earth, the planet filled with Light." However, in general, it can be understood to mean, "the One who exerts His power over the entire Earth, who is working to protect humankind with the power of God."

Earlier, I said that the word "El" is often used to mean God and Light. This linguistic origin also applies to "el" in the name "Israel." "El" in Israel means "God." The name, Israel, comes from Jacob, who became the Patriarch of Israelites. It is said that one night, Jacob wrestled until daybreak with a godlike or angel-like being with wings, whose appearance could barely be seen in the dark. This godlike being was surprised by how well Jacob wrestled and gave him the name, Israel, which means "he who contends with God" or "he who wrestles with God." This is the original meaning behind the name of the country of Israel. The nation's forefather, named Jacob Israel, had wrestled with God.

In this way, El Cantare has various connections and I have started to reveal them little by little. At the end of last year, we recorded a spiritual interview with Rient Arl Croud, an ancient king who lived in South America. It has now been published and made available for anyone to read to gain a better understanding of him and his life. Like so, I plan to put out more spiritual interviews with the soul siblings of El Cantare; to reveal their ideas and what they were like. By publishing spiritual messages of the branch spirits of El Cantare who were born on earth, I am hoping that people can get a deeper understanding of El Cantare as a whole. As for the core consciousness of El Cantare, such as Alpha and Elohim, you will be able to get a better and clearer understanding of them through Happy Science animation movies.

2

The Purpose of Publishing
Spiritual Messages

The Laws of Faith covers many different topics. There is heavy focus on international politics which may be difficult for some readers to follow. However, I feel the need to mention them because the teachings of Happy Science are reaching the world as well. We also carry out political activities, but in reality, our party does not have enough power in the political world as of now. That is why I place more emphasis on foreseeing the future or voicing our opinions to indicate the right direction for the world. And currently, politics is moving in the direction I have been speaking about.

Happy Science has gone through several innovations in terms of how we manage our group and carry out our activities. However, we have yet to reach the level that I hope. Although the number of our staff has exceeded 2,000 people, those who are active in our political party are less than 50. Out of 2,000, a little less than 50 staff members are active in our political wing, so their influential power is only one-twentieth of the group as a whole. This means that we have not even put in one-tenth of our total capability. For this reason, although our members become slightly enthusiastic about our political activity during the busy campaign season, they tend to forget about it most of the time. So, as we continue doing our political activities, we need to increase the number of volunteers who are specifically devoted to political activities. I believe it is difficult for our entire group to focus only on political activities.

Now that over 30 years have passed (since Happy Science was founded), I have come full circle and the generation of our members has changed. So this year, I believe I must return to the starting point of religion and repeatedly teach about the mind and the basics of enlightenment. The younger members have not heard the teachings that I had given in the early days of Happy Science. That is why I would like to go over the basic teachings of religion again and then move on to talk about the laws of faith. Thus, I will be giving more lectures about the mind from different perspectives. We need to encourage younger members from time to time to study the Truth from a beginner's level.

Having said this, I was unable to thoroughly teach about faith back in the early days. As a newly founded religion, it was difficult to strongly emphasize the importance of faith. So I started out by publishing a series of books consisting of spiritual messages received from high spirits. I introduced the words of many Buddhist monks and gods of other religions to help people understand what faith is. It was a way of suggesting to them, "You have faith in these spirits, right? So, from that, please gradually grasp what it means to have faith in religion."

Thus, I published many books of spiritual messages in the beginning. However, as each spirit said different things, we started to add a disclaimer stating that the opinions of these spirits do not necessarily reflect our teachings. This then made people unsure about what to exactly believe in. Spirits in the other world also have the freedom of speech, so they talk about their own ideas. After all, you cannot expect Nichiren to preach the teachings of Shinran, or Shinran to preach the teachings of Nichiren. They each express their own opinions. For this reason, more and more people started requesting theoretical books that contained my thoughts. So from around 1994, I took a break from publishing spiritual message books and focused on publishing more of my own theoretical books.

However, a while after I stopped publishing spiritual messages, some people who liked them started to feel dissatisfied. Then, there was a person who began boasting that she could receive spiritual messages and actually published them as books. Some of our members ended up following that person. Seeing this trend, I felt that I still needed to provide proof that the Spirit World exists, and started publishing many books of spiritual messages again in the last 10 years.

After I stopped publishing them around 1994, we started seeing some people gathering their own followers by saying, "Ryuho Okawa has lost his spiritual powers, so come to us instead." On other occasions, although I had published spiritual messages and specifically expressed that the messages were the opinions of the spirits themselves and were different from mine, people still criticized us and said that we were not a religion. This was a difficult problem. In the end, I decided to provide basic teachings while at the same time, introducing the opinions of spirits as "reference." This is in consideration of those who are involved in or used to believe in different religions.

3

Overcoming Conflicts between Religions

Understanding idol worship

We have members who used to be Christians and Buddhists. There are also many people who are considered the followers of Japanese Shinto, although they themselves are unaware of it. In fact, in Shinto, you are automatically counted as a follower if you simply walk through its *torii* gate. This is especially true if you visit a shrine during the New Year and walk through it. The total number of visitors is what the Association of Shinto Shrines publicizes as the total number of their believers. This is probably why the number fluctuates dramatically depending on the economic situation. They sometimes say they have 96 million believers and at other times 77 million believers, and these are the number of people who have passed through the torii gate in that particular year.

If that is how we can count our believers, then I might as well build many torii gates at Happy Science [*audience laughs*]. However, I believe we should not allow ourselves

69

to choose the easy way. Our local branch managers are required to work at a higher level. It is said that on average, those who pass through a torii gate make an offering of ¥15 (about 10 cents). If so, the total amount of donations will not be much even though millions of people visit Shinto shrines. That is why the total number of believers is not everything. Of course, I have also walked through torii gates, so there is a good chance that I too have been counted as a follower of Japanese Shinto. In any case, every religion has its own practice.

As for myself, I try to repeatedly say what I believe is right. However, that is not to say that all other religions are wrong. I respect other religions and openly accept those who believe in them. They can believe in the teachings of their religions which they find to be helpful. This is my stance. Unless we take this kind of tolerant attitude, I do not think religious conflicts, like those between Christianity and Islam, will end.

Islam wiped out Buddhism from India in the 13th century. And now, in Myanmar, Buddhism and Islam are opposing fiercely. Should the number of Muslims greatly increase in Myanmar, Buddhism might perish there because Muslims believe that idol worship is wrong; they may come to destroy the statues of Buddha. If the statues of Buddha are destroyed, most Buddhist temples and groups will cease to exist. Therefore, even Buddhists tend to strongly dislike the influx of Muslims into their country, which is why there is tension near the border of Myanmar. They are facing immigration problems; even Buddhists are equipping themselves with machine guns.

There is actually no problem with banning idol worship. It is natural to believe that God in heaven cannot be expressed in this material world. So the idea of banning it, itself, is fine and acceptable. However, Muslims should not force their belief on others and destroy the objects of worship of other religions.

In truth, Christianity also thinks that idol worship is wrong. But while they say worshiping an object or a statue is wrong, they accept two-dimensional representations of God. Greek Orthodox Churches, for example, display pictures of Jesus and pictures of Mary. Even so, with the development of sculpture art, many churches began to display the statues of Jesus, Mary, and the Virgin and Child.

After all, human beings need some kind of object to worship. So, it is only natural that each religion has its own unique object and way of expressing its faith. We must be tolerant of this act of worship.

In the case of Islam, a mosque is just a huge open space, and there is virtually nothing inside it. Some of them have holes in the ceiling. You might think that since it has no roof, it is acceptable to enter the building with your hat on, but that is not the case. You will be told to take it off. In this way, each religion has its own manners to be followed. So in principle, it is best to respect the custom of each place of worship and think that what you believe in your mind is a different matter.

As I wrote in *The Laws of Faith*, some founders of religions had the ability to hear God's voice or write revelations from God through automatic writing. Yet, they did not have the spiritual sight to see God or angels while they were alive. These types of religions tend to denounce idol worship. But the truth was that those founders simply did not talk about things that they did not experience. Their followers just take it to mean that what their founders did not mention are things they were prohibited from doing.

Happy Science teaches
how to remove your attachments

Although there are many teachings at Happy Science, they essentially align very closely with the teachings of Buddhism. But I have to say, even Buddhist teachings are not complete. In general, Buddhism is a little indifferent toward worldly matters and slightly detached from this earthly life due to the belief that the goal is to transcend this world. That attitude is right in itself, but now that the human lifespan is getting longer, we should not take life in this world so lightly.

Of course, if your attachment to this world grows to the point that you begin to think that this world is your eternal home, then you have gone too far; it will become difficult for you to return to heaven after death. That is why I teach you how you can remove your attachments using the Buddhist approach.

4

The Mindset Toward
Prayer and Miracles

Build a strong connection with God
while making diligent efforts

I also teach about the power of prayer. However, if you overly use prayer to only achieve prosperity in this world, your spirituality will be lost. You can use prayer in the hope of solving worldly problems, but there are times when things do not turn out the way you want in this world. Therefore, I am always thinking about the importance of prayer and how it should be taught, so that people can smoothly return to the other world.

Christianity is commonly known as a religion that holds faith in the Other-Power, but even so, they still expect their believers to make their own efforts. It takes self-discipline and effort to study the Bible, say prayers, or take action, and Christians believe that this Self-Power is always supported by the power of God or Jesus.

In Christianity today, Jesus is sometimes referred to as "God" or "Lord" and there is virtually no distinction between Jesus and God, which I guess cannot be helped. Christians believe that they are connected with Jesus or God through prayer. So when they fight devils, they will do so with God, and when they make a mistake, they will ask for God's forgiveness. In this way, Christians build a connection with the other world and make efforts in their spiritual practice. Fortunately, this means spirituality still remains in certain areas of Christian practice.

Recently, however, churches are losing against the material development of this world. As a result, miracles rarely occur; so, Christianity is also going through difficult times. Hospitals are full of people with materialistic ways of thinking, and churches are also unable to reach out to these people, either. Unfortunately, nothing can be done about this. Of course, you can treat your illness through medical technology and cure what you can, but sometimes, there are too many misunderstandings in medical treatment. What I mean to say is that there are a great number of symptoms whose causes are unknown or cannot be medically explained. In such cases, doctors often give some kind of a name to a symptom or suggest a potential cause, but many cases remain a mystery to them.

When you find yourself in such situations, it is also important to examine your connection with God once again. If there are mistakes in your way of life and you have problems of your own or have family issues, then you should reexamine them. You should reflect on yourself in front of God and try to correct your future actions. This type of effort is essential.

By making these efforts, many people at Happy Science have actually experienced miracles, such as complete recovery from illnesses. If testimonies like these were made into a movie, it would be a great collection of miracles[2]. Considering the fact that even Christians hardly admit the miracles happening at Lourdes, it is difficult to make ordinary people believe in them. However, many miracles are happening in reality.

Although I mainly teach the importance of Self-Power at Happy Science, what comes first is for you to build a close relationship with God and make efforts based on it. It is certainly true that your thoughts will manifest themselves, so you can of course achieve your goal by dint of your power of thoughts. But if you focus only on yourself, you may end up becoming someone like a worldly salesperson who solely prays to raise their sales record. But it is extremely important to remember that humans have a higher purpose than this.

El Cantare was the Father in Heaven who guided Jesus

Christians today are confused as to whether Jesus is God or not, or the Lord or not. As a matter of fact, just like how it is written clearly in the Bible, there was the Father in Heaven and Jesus was able to hear His words. At times, the Father in Heaven was helping Jesus when he performed miracles and healed the sick, and imbued power in Jesus' words when he was giving a sermon. You can probably understand this clearly by looking at the phenomena occurring at Happy Science. So, Jesus and the Father in Heaven are different existences.

Actually, the Father in Heaven who was guiding Jesus at the time was El Cantare. This is what I am conveying.

So far, we have never received any criticism about this from any Christian churches or Christians. They may have accepted this as the truth, or perhaps they may be dismissing it. I am not sure about this. The total number of Christians in Japan is said to be less than one percent of the population, so they may simply be keeping silent, thinking that they are too small a group [compared to Happy Science]. Perhaps when the leader of our political party, the Happiness Realization Party, gets elected as the prime minister, they may start criticizing us severely. But since it may still take some time for this to come true, I think I am safe to say it for the time being. I, myself, talk very openly and frankly about the Truth that I must teach.

Using prayer as the final step

Miracles sometimes happen and sometimes do not. There is no fixed or absolute rule in this regard. Miracles are rare occurrences; they only occur to help you believe that there might be a power beyond this world. If miracles occur all the time without fail, then the world we live in will lose its significance; there will be no purpose as to why the third dimensional world exists separately from the other dimensions. That is why miracles do not happen so frequently.

If humans become lazy and learn the easy way, they may go as far as to ask God to turn the lights off in their rooms. Yet, God would say, "Get your act together. Get on your feet and turn it off yourself." In other words, you should not use prayer to fix all of your problems. You are expected to do what you can on your own. However, when you have come to a dead end and are at a complete loss as to what to do, or when you are feeling distressed and troubled, then you can use prayer. At that time, God will help you open up a way.

You should not ask, "Oh God, I don't have any instant noodles to eat today. I'll leave the necessary ingredients here, so please turn them into noodles." He would surely say, "I'm busy." Basically, that is not how things work. You will have to do it yourself. However, when you have lost your job, have no income, and are struggling to make a living, then you can turn to prayer. Of course, you should make the effort to go job hunting and do what you can, but if you pray, you will be filled with power. You can, for example, say in your prayer, "God, I believe I have a mission in life and I definitely want to fulfill it, but I don't have enough financial power to achieve it right now. Please help me so that I can meet good people, find a good job, and accomplish greater work." Then, when the time is right, someone will surely appear before you and help you. Even in this day and age, I think about one out of ten people is spiritually sensitive. So, if you ask for help through prayer, someone will somehow sense it and come to you. If you are in a difficult situation, pray to El Cantare and other high spirits so that they can call on people who can help you. Happy Science conducts many ritual prayers, so if you pray, I am sure a path will open up before you.

5

Miracles Require Diligent Effort

The secret that keeps Happy Science going for more than 30 years

Many company owners will probably experience various hardships and setbacks from now on. Indeed, they will have a tough time running their businesses. I heard just yesterday that only one in 5,000 companies can survive for more than 30 years. Although Happy Science is not a company, we have made it into our 32nd year since its establishment (at the time of the lecture). We are one of the one-in-5,000 that have survived and are still continuing to work hard. We also have IRH Press, which is a limited liability company, and it has successfully made it through as one of the one-in-5,000 companies as well. Therefore, our organization should not be underestimated.

Publishing companies in Japan such as *Bungeishunju* and *Shinchosha* are managing their businesses by having many outsourced writers and in-house writers. *Kodansha*, which is a far larger publishing company, has 1,000 employees and they are just about sustained by 10,000 writers. Compared to this, although IRH Press publishes books written by other authors as well, it is virtually sustained by a single author. We have survived in this way for over 30 years. This shows that we are not just merely on the level of being one-in-5,000 surviving companies, but are experiencing a miracle of much smaller chance.

Other publishing companies may find this to be quite an unbelievable feat; they are envious of a religion that can make such things happen. That is why they criticize us, but half of what they write is likely to be out of jealousy. Therefore, it is probably best not to take it word for word. People working at these publishing companies struggle to approach and urge many writers to write for them. Unfortunately, they have difficulty collecting their manuscripts every week. On the contrary, we are fortunate to be able to publish books one after another without ever having to go through all that trouble. They are probably frustrated seeing us publish more than a hundred books a year in such a way. I do feel very sorry for them, but there is no other way to put it but to say this is the power of

God. I do not think there has ever been anyone who tried to demonstrate God's power through diligent work.

I believe diligence is also one's strength. If I were lazy, it would not have been possible to publish this many books. So, I think diligence is a form of power. Even if well-known authors wish to go independent and start publishing their own monthly magazines, three issues are usually the most they can publish. This is the general case. In our case, ever since we started publishing monthly magazines at Happy Science, I have never once had trouble writing a manuscript, and neither have I ever been pressed for one. This is only natural to us, but at the same time, I am very grateful for being able to do this. This has been made possible due to my own efforts as well as the great amount of support I receive from heaven. The great power from the "ocean" of infinite wisdom that I receive is largely the reason I am able to continue my work. No matter how many times I humbly express my gratitude, I do not think it will ever be enough.

Since I am still under spiritual training, I sometimes worry whether I am speaking too highly of myself. Even so, I suspect that other religious leaders are very lenient in their spiritual discipline, though I do not mean to overstep. Since there are over 180,000 religious groups in Japan, I am not fully aware of all of their activities. If they are not receiving much guidance from God or Buddha, perhaps more effort is required. I believe that as long as you are making enough effort earnestly, diligently, and in a respectable way, you will naturally be given positive results.

Continually ask yourself
if you have made progress today

Many miracles are happening all around us. Our movement itself is a miracle. The fact that you are all living; you are able to do various jobs; we are able to do our missionary activities in this country as well as overseas. These are all miracles in themselves, and they are actually the result of people with faith making diligent efforts upon efforts without wasting a single day.

The proof that you are a child of God is to make each day of your life shine brilliantly. You should sometimes have ambitious goals and create strategies to realize them, especially on occasions like the New Year. These efforts are essential, but more importantly, you need to take a step forward every day and ask yourself time and again, "Did I make any progress today?" This is the secret to advancing in life.

This lecture is said to be my 2,700th lecture, but this number only includes the ones that have been made public. In reality, there are many more that have not been released. The total number of lectures I gave last year (2017) is publically known to be 132. Aside from those, there were some additional 300 unofficial recordings. These unofficial recordings are mostly personal life counseling as well as advice from high spirits on our internal matters that are causing us problems, confusion, and troubles. They are recordings that not all people need to listen to and are preferred to be kept confidential. This is why we do not release them. So although we have reported 132 as the official number of lectures I gave that year, there were roughly more than 300 unofficial recordings in that year alone.

Thus, there are many more lectures that have been recorded behind the scenes. These unofficial recordings actually work like secret ingredient; you can "get the flavor" of it in my lectures that are released to the public. They are sometimes made available to our staff members or exclusively to executives. Apparently, when our executives or branch managers give a lecture, they sometimes include the information they had received from those unofficial recordings. Our members will sometimes hear about things they have never heard of and find the lecturer grinning a little during their speech; this is usually one of those cases. These unofficial lectures also work as materials for the lectures I give at public venues.

Keep fighting to accomplish something year after year

My humble goal for this year is to exceed a total of 2,800 lectures[3]. I ask you all to please follow me. Let us keep advancing forward.

We must keep advancing! There is no regressing.

I have returned to the starting point of religion to teach about the matters of the mind once again. We are also trying to further expand Happy Science with the help of volunteer members under a low-cost management system. A weekly magazine that is on the brink of going bankrupt is saying that Happy Science is on the decline, but that is absolutely not true. The figure they are describing is completely off. I want to say to them, "The figure you say is the sales of your company. I don't want you to think that we are the same."

Happy Science is aiming to advance forward. I am now hoping to involve the new generation more so that we can launch an even larger movement. I will do my best to exceed a total of 2,800 lectures this year. I would also like you all to keep on fighting year after year so that you can say, "This year, I accomplished this and that" every year, and leave behind brilliant achievements.

EDITOR'S NOTES

1 Ryuho Okawa is the executive producer and has written the original story of all three movies, *The Laws of the Universe - Part 0*, *I* and *II*.

2 Later, the documentary film, *Living in the Age of Miracles* was released (original concept by Ryuho Okawa).

3 This was achieved in September 2018.

CHAPTER THREE

Choose Light over Darkness

—Living a Life of Service to the World—

Recorded in Japanese on March 14, 2020
at Happy Science Sendai Shoshinkan in Miyagi Prefecture.
English translation.

1

The Meaning of Trials that Humankind Faces

Unexpected misfortunes teach humans lessons

It is good to see everyone again. It has been a long time since I last visited Sendai. I presume people living in other areas in this Tohoku region (North East Japan), are also watching this lecture (via satellite). You must have been going through many kinds of hardships and painful experiences, so I hope my visit will encourage you, even by just a little.

As you all know, [due to the coronavirus pandemic] many places are closing down, and many events are being canceled one after the other. People are being told not to hold any community gatherings. Even the National High School Baseball Championship was canceled and the Sumo Wrestling Tournament was held without an audience. People are now saying that the Tokyo Olympics could be canceled and the government is discussing whether or not it should be postponed for one year (at the time of the lecture). But they need to take action more boldly than this.

Unfortunate events have been happening continually, but from the Buddhist perspective, that is life. Life comes with various hardships and difficulties. If life in this world was only filled with happiness, Buddhism would have perished long ago. Because people go through many painful experiences and have many worries, they turn to God or Buddha and find faith for the first time. That is why people sometimes experience events that seem unfair or unreasonable from a worldly perspective. Many people may believe that humankind has been steadily progressing, but sometimes events that are beyond the imagination of experts occur. That is when people realize for the first time how vulnerable human beings are.

When humans mistakenly believe that they have control over nature and have completely unraveled the domains of God, disasters that are beyond human control can occur and people suffer all kinds of misfortunes. Those who have experienced these misfortunes will, of course, go through adversities. But when viewed from a long-term global perspective, such disastrous times are a test for humans to see whether they have become conceited, or have forgotten their original mission.

Humble yourself before a Greater Being

Just three days ago, many events marking the ninth anniversary of the 3/11 Great East Japan Earthquake were held. Nearly 20,000 people died or went missing in this tragic event. But as the Buddhist teachings say, all things are transient. Neither those who have survived nor those who passed on can remain on earth forever. Some may have been happy to have left this world early while those who survived may live on to experience further difficulties. Therefore, it is not so simple to determine your happiness or unhappiness in life.

When humans become arrogant after achieving a pinnacle of civilization in some way, they usually experience natural disasters that they never imagined would occur. It could be an earthquake, tsunami, or storm and flood damage like the one caused by the typhoon last year. This has always been the case in any age. Incidents that destroy human arrogance will happen. Civilization from the 20th century to the 21st century has significantly contributed to the growth of materialism. Furthermore, people begin to believe that science is the only legitimate academic study and nothing else and that scientific technology is the only useful knowledge of humankind. When people become conceited to this level, disastrous events will unfold to cripple their arrogance. Unexpected events will occur, and every time, humanity will be plunged into the depths of despair. The history of humankind seems to repeat itself in this manner. Catastrophes and natural disasters often occur when humanity has wrong value standards or when numerous major conflicts or wars break out due to wrong value judgments. This has actually been the case every time.

It is indeed disheartening when misfortunes happen, but we must not let them defeat us. It is our mission to rise again with strength. Moreover, we must also remain humble amid misfortune and be in awe of the Great Power that is beyond reach or comprehension. Natural disasters can work to wash away trivial evils as well as to "clean" or purify this world on a bigger scale. There is a huge difference between what humans think and what God thinks regarding the direction in which Japan or the whole world should head, from a macro perspective. If human beings cannot fill this gap no matter how much they rack their brain, then they need to thoroughly examine why. Please think once again, whether you were able to humble yourself before a Greater Being.

2

An Age When a Savior Is Born

Severe trials await humankind when the world population increases rapidly

The challenge we currently face is the worldwide spread of pneumonia and pneumonia-caused deaths, triggered by coronavirus infections that originated in China. The World Health Organization (WHO) has declared the coronavirus infection as an unstoppable pandemic that is impacting the whole world. Naturally, newspapers and weekly magazines have been writing about a potential great depression that may take place on a global scale. The situation may be unfavorable in the short-term perspective; but from the long-term perspective, considering what humankind has done in recent centuries, it would be wise to perceive this situation as a type of warning.

At the beginning of the 20th century, the world population was still small—between 1 to 2 billion. Around the time when I started giving public lectures, it increased to 5 billion. A little later, I remember saying that it was 5.2 billion, then 6 billion, and now it is approaching 8 billion. However, I do not think the world population will keep on growing at this pace. I believe there will be conflicts along the way before it reaches 10 billion. I have been assuming for a long time that some type of severe hardship will befall humankind.

Furthermore, there is something I do not want the Japanese people to misunderstand. They may optimistically think that now that the Savior is born, things will only turn for the better. However, according to what is commonly understood in Western society, a savior is only born in an era when great disasters happen and the world seems to be ending. It is said that a savior is born only when humans have truly become helpless and are plunged into despair as the result of catastrophes, such as the destruction of a whole country or the collapse of a civilization.

While Japanese people would celebrate the birth of a savior, people in other countries would hesitate to accept this, but this is not to say that other countries lack faith. It is because they know that a savior's descent also means that catastrophes are imminent. This is a common view in Western society.

As for the scale of these disasters, you will witness it in the near future.

Do not forget that the coronavirus infection originated in China

According to the official statement, the number of people infected with the coronavirus has now exceeded 100,000, and more than 5,000 people have died from it (at the time of the lecture). However, this number is what the government officials have grasped from existing hospital records. In reality, some people have died before being tested at the hospital and being hospitalized. Some have even died from being diagnosed with other diseases. So the true number is estimated to be far bigger than this. According to spiritual messages I have taken, the number of victims is anticipated to be astronomical. One hundred thousand infections and 5,000 deaths are not astronomical numbers, so I believe we will not be able to stop the pandemic by simply, for example, closing schools and businesses for two weeks or canceling concerts and gatherings.

Now that the pandemic spread throughout the world, people are gradually forgetting how it all started and are beginning to feel that it is just a virus that is everywhere in the world. As I wrote in my book, the coronavirus infection started in China[1]. Please do not forget this.

The Chinese spokesperson recently changed his statement completely and started saying that a coronavirus variant started in Japan and is now spreading globally. They are trying to make it as though the coronavirus originated in Japan and make the world believe it. Yet, a few days ago, the Chinese spokesperson started mentioning the possibility of the pandemic being a virus attack on Wuhan by the U.S. military. Perhaps China was reacting sharply to the recent remarks that were made by a high-ranking U.S. official. I am amazed at how sly they can be, but this is their usual tactic.

In the beginning, China laudably admitted its responsibility and humbly expressed regret. However, once the pandemic spread around the world and more countries were marked in "red" on the world map that tracked the spreading of the coronavirus infections, it became difficult to tell where the virus first derived. China even said that it might have been the U.S. military that attacked them with a biological weapon. They use such logic to evade responsibility, which is a bit shocking. In this way, if the pandemic continues for a long time, the original cause may become ambiguous.

However, as far as I understand, the pandemic started when the virus was somehow leaked from a bioweapons research institute in Wuhan, China. I stated this clearly in my books, which is now cited in various media outlets. This may be why China became desperate and started mentioning the possible attack from the U.S. In addition, this could mean that Happy Science is influencing the world behind the scenes. I hope people will observe these things objectively without getting emotionally affected.

Nevertheless, it does not mean you should hate the Chinese people. I am simply saying that there are problems within China's political system. China conceals and manipulates information on an incredible scale. They have gotten used to manipulating and concealing figures and information because all their news media are government-owned. However, they should know that such tactics will not work now that they have affected the whole world.

China may continue to evade responsibility by saying that another country is responsible for the pandemic. But if they start blaming the pandemic on Japan, that will be troubling for us.

China should have the WHO inspect the Wuhan Institute of Virology and have them openly report it on camera before they make their claims. If China does not allow any investigations, they are in no position to blame other countries. At the very least, it was in Wuhan that the infection first spread and it was the Beijing government that shut down the city with over 10 million people. They must have known that a serious accident occurred there but they concealed it. Although they initially expected the infection to subside quickly, it spread so widely that they could no longer hide it. So they had no choice but to take measures to stop it. This was the course of the event, and we should know this.

I am not saying that the Chinese people are to blame. I am saying that there are problems with the ruling regime that is suppressing them. The Chinese government should inform its people of the truth more, and it needs to be more accountable especially because this issue has affected the entire world.

A battle between the "communist virus" and "faith immunity"

In the beginning, the Japanese government banned people from Hubei Province from entering Japan but still allowed Chinese people from other places to come in. But when China and South Korea started to ban Japanese citizens from entering their countries, the Japanese government realized that the tables had turned and they quickly tightened their policies.

However, by the time the Chinese government placed a lockdown in Wuhan, which originally had a population of about 11 million people, there were only about 5 million residents left in the city. By then, the other 6 million people had already fled to other regions in China. Because they were still able to enter Japan from areas outside of Hubei Province at the time, they managed to flee to other countries by passing through Japan. Many Chinese people traveled to other countries in this way, which is one of the reasons why the infection spread all across the world.

In this sense, unfortunately, the Japanese government was too late in taking countermeasures. I must say that they prioritized economic gain. Perhaps it could not have been helped to some extent as it was an unprecedented event. But even so, Japan should be able to defend itself.

In any case, I do not think that a mere two-week restriction on people's activities will settle the issue. The infection will most probably spread even further. As we always say at Happy Science, this is actually a battle between the "materialism and atheism gene," namely the "communist virus," and "faith immunity" or "faith antibody." Please know this. It would be a huge problem if the atheistic and materialistic ways of thinking prevailed and took over the world.

The number of infected cases increased tremendously even in Italy, where the Vatican is located. This is partly because the Pope succumbed to China's political power and failed to guide Christians in China under their faith. In addition, Italy's decision to rely on the Chinese economy and to support the Belt and Road Initiative led to a large influx of people from China, and this also helped spread the infection within their country. South Korea suffered a lot as a result of relying heavily on China as well.

The pandemic will continue for a while. We can no longer carry out activities in the same way as we have been doing until now. Regardless, we must have a strong will to start again from scratch. People were helpless when the Great East Japan Earthquake hit their region, but over time, they gradually got back on their feet. Some venture businesses have now started up in the Tohoku region. Similarly, when the atomic bomb was dropped on Hiroshima, people believed that it was the end of the world, but even so, they beautifully rebuilt their region. Moreover, when Kobe suffered the most from the Great Hanshin Earthquake and people thought that it could no longer function, the city managed to revive completely. So, although disasters sometimes happen and seemingly unreasonable events occur, disaster-stricken areas can be restored and become even more powerful than before.

3

Japan, Be an Independent Country

Do what you can every day even during the pandemic

What I want to tell you is this: The damage caused by the coronavirus will continue to spread more on a global scale, so you should not think optimistically that the pandemic will subside in a short period, or it is not long until things will go back to normal, for example, by the end of March. An economic downturn, or an economic crisis similar to the Great Depression, will probably occur down the line.

As for the economy, the Japanese government hiked up the consumption tax rate to 10 percent last October (2019). I told them not to do it numerous times, but they did not listen to my advice. That is why we are now in a difficult situation. Please know this. The "rosy future" that the Japanese government was hoping for did not happen. Back then, I said that it was not the right time to raise the consumption tax rate because it would prevent the Japanese economy from making a full recovery. But now, the situation is so dire that recovering it is out of the question.

At the "El Cantare Celebration" last December, I clearly warned people of the potential danger of a great economic depression that would start in China and might damage Japan, and indeed, this became a reality. However, we cannot change what has already happened, so we must now restart our lives by doing what we can every day. People in the past were much poorer and they suffered through much more miserable times. During the Great Depression in the late 1920s to early 1930s, people's lives were difficult in the Tohoku region. Back then, many people starved to death and parents even had to sell their children. Humankind experienced such harsh times. But we must continue moving forward by overcoming these tough times repeatedly and learning lessons from them. So, now is the time to return to the starting point once again and think about what we can do.

Raise the self-sufficiency rate in food and energy, and create production systems

What we especially need to consider now is the following point: People used to think that economic trade makes the world run smoothly and that as long as there are no wars, the economy will only develop. But now, this basic premise is starting to collapse and conflicts are occurring in many places. As a result, materials that we had been importing from foreign countries are no longer available and materials that we were hoping to export can no longer be sold. Some companies are experiencing difficulties as they can no longer purchase specific parts for their machine from overseas to make their products. These problems have been occurring a lot, but what are they teaching us? They are teaching us to reexamine whether we can stay independent as a country in case of an emergency.

In particular, Japan's food self-sufficiency rate is currently below 40 percent. Areas like the Tohoku region, for example, should think about creating systems that will supply enough food for the Japanese citizens in case Japan becomes unable to import food from other countries.

Japan should reassess how their agriculture and fishing industry should operate.

In the manufacturing industry, too, many companies open their factories in foreign countries that have low labor costs. They then import the parts manufactured there and assemble the products in Japan. Until now, businesses have only been concerned about making profits by selling cheaply made products that supply domestic needs. But now, they must think about relocating their factories to rural areas in Japan and creating new jobs there. This way, they can hire many locals. Establishing a system like this is extremely important and necessary to maintain Japan as an independent country. This is not merely an issue of labor cost. If many countries start to ban the entry of foreign nationals, we will not be able to conduct any trade or make business contracts anymore; Japan was not thinking about this possibility.

So Japan should work to increase the food self-sufficiency rate and create systems to manufacture products that are entirely made in Japan. We must do our best to avoid a situation in which a foreign energy supply shortage stops Japan from functioning. So it is more important to figure out how to increase the energy self-sufficiency rate than worrying about the cost that it entails. Modern civilization will collapse if the energy supply stops, so Japan must overcome this issue at any cost.

Japan must voice its opinions against what is wrong

I have been voicing various opinions for more than 10 years now, but the people in mass media and politics do not seem to understand what I mean. It seems as though they cannot understand what we are saying.

I have also been warning about the North Korean issue for a long time. Even while the whole world is in huge shock and is experiencing a great economic downturn that was caused by the coronavirus pandemic, North Korea continues to casually fire missiles and conduct weapons tests. It is such an eccentric country that it makes me want to say that the whole country should "time travel" elsewhere or teleport itself to another planet in the universe. Although, I do pity the country.

Japan must be able to clearly state what is wrong as wrong. It must not be a country that cannot speak up. This may be a sore point for the Japanese government, but Japan must become a country that can voice opinions more strongly. To do so, it is fundamental that Japan restores its power. Some statistics predict that by 2050, Japan will fall below the top 20 in the world's GDP ranking, but it should not simply accept this. Rather, it should refute such a prediction and say, "No, that is not right. We will take on the challenge to rise to an even higher position from our current ranking as third place (at the time of the lecture)." Japan needs to have this kind of strong will to revive its economy.

4

The New Teachings that Will Guide the World to a Better Future

The world is now at a crossroads to choose between light and darkness

The greatest reason why Japan must become strong is that new teachings that will guide the world to a brighter future are now being taught here, in this 21st century. Happy Science is trying to overcome conflicts between religions and different races or between people of different skin colors. Our teachings are now spreading. People should be aware of this fact more clearly. Happy Science is still far from being well-known in the world. Even in Japan, many have heard of the name but do not understand the difference between Happy Science and other religious groups. This is a shame.

To be blunt, unless you can bravely say, "Japanese people, El Cantare has now descended in Japan. Follow His guiding hand!" Japan will only keep declining. The question is, will people of later generations learn about His descent in history? Or will people awaken and follow Him in this age, today?

It has already been 39 years since I first received revelations from heaven (at the time of the lecture). I have been carrying out this movement for 39 years. My determination has never once changed. I am an honest man. I do not compromise easily. I stick to what I believe is right. But despite working for 39 years, Japan has yet to awaken. In that case, we must keep on trying and make further efforts.

A book that was published recently said that Happy Science only has 13,000 members. But that is not true; when I went to Nepal to give a lecture, we already had over 70,000 local members[2]. We also built a large *shoja* there. When the big earthquake hit Nepal, many people came to rely on Happy Science. So Happy Science is spreading around the world as well. Even so, I hope that our main ground Japan will be stronger and have a greater influential power. And I hope you, too, will do your best to make it happen. No matter how much I raise my voice alone, it will not be enough to make Japan stronger.

In this small society and market of Japan, Happy Science has been the target of jealousy from other publishing companies and religious groups. But we should not be defeated by their trifling envy. We have a duty to achieve far greater success. Unless we achieve bigger success, we will not be able to save the world. People of other religious groups may feel offended to see that we have grown bigger than them or that we have built bigger facilities than theirs, but this achievement is still small compared to our aspirations. We must be known to a far greater number of people. I want people to know this.

The world is now at a crossroads to choose between light and darkness. It is our duty to indicate what is light and what is darkness. I have already taught about this in many different ways for over 30 years, but my teachings have yet to reach the world fully. Of course, freedom of speech is very important. However, please know that although there are various opinions in the world, it does not mean that it is right to adopt any of them. You must choose what is right. There are many different ways of thinking, but God or Buddha clearly has a certain way of thinking that He wants humans to choose. I want people to know this.

Happy Science teachings can be summed up in four principles

Our basic teachings are founded upon faith in El Cantare. This Spiritual Being has worked to create many world religions and civilizations on Earth and is now trying to bestow His teachings in this world. So we must spread them so that humans can live by the teachings. These teachings can otherwise be explained as the "right mind humans should have," which can be summed up in the four principles of love, wisdom, self-reflection, and progress.

The first is the Principle of Love, which is about giving love to others. People generally believe that love is to receive or to take, but that is not true. If you believe that love is to take, you will start hating the person you love when he or she does not love you back. Your love will turn to hatred when you cannot receive the love you sought for. This is the kind of love that is often observed in the world. But you will not feel that way if you practice "love that gives." This is the Principle of Love.

The second is the Principle of Wisdom. What is taught in academia and school education has largely changed in the last 100 to 200 years. Some people say that ever since humans were disenchanted with the belief in magic and liberated themselves from the control of churches, they have become free in human society. While there is some truth in this idea, knowledge and education should never sever the tie between God and His children, namely humans. It is certainly important to use our wisdom to create a better society, but if modern people start denying the existence of God who stands above them, they must accept the negative repercussions to come. I believe we need to teach this to people.

The third is the Principle of Self-Reflection. Unlike Western religions or mainly Christianity, I do not teach that once people make a mistake, they will inevitably go to hell and can never return to heaven. Although people do make mistakes, they can get back on their feet by awakening to their Buddha-nature through self-reflection. Even those who have fallen to hell can be saved by this Principle of Self-Reflection. You can help the spirits in hell, including your ancestors, to get back on their feet by studying Buddha's Truth and offering them guidance while on earth. This is what I teach in the Principle of Self-Reflection.

Lastly, in the Principle of Progress, I teach that utopia on earth is not only about attaining material abundance and development but also about achieving progress and prosperity that incorporate Buddha's Truth. What I mean by creating utopia on earth is creating the Kingdom of God in this world. It is the world that reflects the Will of God.

In the process of achieving this, I may sometimes give harsh criticisms about some countries. However, please do not misunderstand the direction in which I am guiding humanity. If you only think about the development of this earthly world, you may only need to think materialistically and believe that science is almighty. But the utopia I speak of must incorporate something that transcends material development.

Having said this, however, we are by no means recommending people to go back to living primitively. We agree and support the idea of developing maglev trains, for example. In that sense, our ideas are in line with worldly, materialistic, scientific, and technological development. We want to become "the beacon of the lighthouse" that will guide the world by producing more wealth and paving the way for the poor to prosper. That is why we need to spread our teachings all over the world, and to do so, Japan, the starting point of our movement, must regain its power and keep progressing powerfully.

Gain the power to break the norms of the era

When we are born into this world, we live in a physical body. In this sense, unfortunately, my activities in this world are limited. This third dimensional world has its own laws, so there is a limit to what I can do. But each one of you also has the power as a child of God or Buddha. Therefore, I want you to exert your full power to fight, prosper, and keep making efforts to create a true Buddha Land utopia for the coming age. It is important for those who have awakened to faith to create an advanced, prosperous nation based on faith. The development and prosperity I speak of encompasses art, as well. As introduced earlier, we also promote artistic activities so that we can convey our teachings even to those who do not read books[3].

In addition, we have been carrying out political activities for more than 10 years now, though we are still unable to show our true potential. Japan is a strange country where people neglect the candidates who assert the right opinions while accepting the ones who lie to win many votes. People are well aware that certain candidates are lying, but they willingly get fooled and even enjoy being deceived. There are many people like this. To add, the police would crack down on trivial violations of the election law but overlook big illegal events. For example, they allow a cherry blossom-viewing cocktail party to be held at a luxury hotel for 15,000 guests from rural regions. The participants may enjoy the event and it may, indeed, be a utopia for the political party hosting it.

However, there is something wrong with a society that allows particular politicians to confidently practice such bribery during the non-election period; and they can even be exempt from taking responsibility if they pretend to know nothing about it. The mass media is lenient on them, too. You must be able to think that this is wrong. If you are involved in political campaigns and were to give ¥1,000 (about $6) to voters, you would be arrested straight away, but if a group of politicians openly invite people to a cherry blossom viewing party and play innocent about it, they can evade responsibility. This is not fair. The Public Offices Election Act is supposed to realize a fair election, but it does not. It only works to protect the establishment.

For this reason, we need to adopt a more "Rock 'n' Roll" attitude. By this, I mean we should break the norms of the era. When we find something wrong in what is commonly accepted, we should break it. I believe we need to have the power to do so.

We must also tell people the true meaning of "Love & Peace." What we mean by love is different from what is commonly believed. What we mean by peace is different from what is upheld by the leftists. The "peace" advocated by the leftists in Japan is based on a self-deprecating view of history. It is as if they are saying, "Please invade our country as you please" to other nations. Their idea of peace may even jeopardize the independence of other foreign countries that have followed Japan as a model. Our ideas are different from these leftists'. We are asserting that we must create an independent country, respect each other's culture, and get along with other countries based on chivalry. But if some countries commit wrongdoings, we should clearly point them out. We need to build a nation that has real power to do so, and of course, this does not mean we should be aggressive toward other countries.

As I said earlier, there is no reason why Japan should be accused of spreading the coronavirus that has gone around the world. The leftists may simply agree on such a statement to keep peace, but we need to be strong. Please also know that divine punishment does occur in reality. It is wrong to believe that humans can change the world however they like. There is a "vaccine" to counter their selfish thoughts and actions. We need to tell people this truth.

5

Keep Fighting through Trials and Never Let Go of Your Hopes

The reason why people of Uyghur, Taiwan, and Hong Kong are counting on Happy Science

We, Happy Science, should not be content with what we have achieved so far. People still take us lightly. We need to be more "explosive" in carrying out our activities. There are over 70,000 believers in Nepal alone. Nepal only has three TV broadcasting stations including a national broadcasting station, and the lecture I gave in Nepal was aired live on two of them. It was aired all around the country. When I gave a lecture in Africa, too, it was aired on TV numerous times for those who missed seeing it that day. In Japan, five or six local TV stations air my lectures, and some newspapers write about them. This current lecture will also be in the newspaper. Compared to other religious groups, we are certainly distinguished, but this achievement is far from what we are aiming for.

When I gave a lecture in New York in 2016, a former news reporter for the *Financial Times*—a British financial and economic paper—came to attend my lecture. He actually interviewed me 30 years ago when he was stationed in Japan; he devoted an entire page of the *Financial Times* to write an article titled, "Japan bows to a new god." He wrote about my lecture at Tokyo Dome, where I spoke to an audience of 50,000 people. He commented that even Jesus Christ would not have been able to give a sermon to such a large number of people. He is currently the CEO of a media group in the U.S. Those who say good things about me surely climb the ladder of success to the top. He is actually Australian. He attended my lecture at Tokyo Dome in 1991 and clearly stated that it was the size of an event that already surpassed any sermon given by Jesus. He wrote that Japanese people were beginning to bow to a new god.

He coined the name, Happy Science. He literally translated the Japanese name, *Kofuku-no-Kagaku*, and called it Happy Science. I had completely forgotten about this and also came up with the same English name myself, but in New York, he thanked me for using the name he thought of.

In 1991, I gave a lecture at Tokyo Dome, and now, we have reached a level where my lectures are being broadcast live to about 3,500 locations around the world. Even so, I believe we need more power to maintain, strengthen, and expand our activities on earth. I have no intention of eliminating Japanese Shinto, Buddhism, Christianity, or Islam. We are simply teaching the modern meaning behind what their founders taught. We are teaching how their founders' teachings should be understood in this modern age.

Although Japanese people are not familiar with Islam, even Muslims have now come to rely on Happy Science. The Muslims living in the Xinjiang Uyghur Autonomous Region in China have come to us for help because they believe that Happy Science is their last resort. They also reached out to us when I went to Canada to give a lecture. They said that the Japanese government would not lend them an ear even though they asked them for help and that we are their last hope. People of Taiwan came to us for help, too, asking for our advice on how they should protect themselves from the potential invasion by China. People of Hong Kong asked us for help, as well. We are being relied on from various places.

Be more "Rock 'n' Roll" and break through the barriers

We are trying to change the value judgment of the world. To our members around the world, I say to you: Be more "Rock 'n' Roll" and break through the barriers [*audience applauds*]. Considering the average age of the audience, I guess many of you are from the Beatles generation. I believe it is time we bravely break through our limits.

Some politicians are just trying to protect their established interests and will even lie to do so, while the mass media act as if they are criticizing the government, but are in fact colluding with politicians. Almost all mass media outlets only curry favor with the government. We must break apart their relationship and tell them, "This is the real Truth. To those who go against it, don't ever think you can stay in power for long." We must be young at heart and raise our spirits to be able to say such things to them. To the people of older generations, I say to you: Do not let the younger ones make light of you! [*Audience applauds.*]

I think young people are making light of the elderly too much—this is especially true in the Tohoku region. You must scold them and say, "We have more wisdom and experience. Listen carefully to the opinions of those who have learned more!" It is said that people will live up to 100 years old starting from the 21st century and onward, so you cannot retire so easily.

Of course, I do not mean to tell young people to keep their mouths shut and do nothing. Those of you who are young should put your blood, sweat, and tears into your work. And if you have extra energy, convey the Truth to others more powerfully. At the same time, be grateful for your parents who raised you and your grandparents and ancestors who supported you. People who do not have this feeling of gratitude cannot be called human; I especially want to emphasize this point to the people in the Tohoku region. Teaching this heart of gratitude is the main road of religion. For younger people to live rightly, they must be grateful to their parents, grandparents, and ancestors, and give back to them as well as to society. It is important to have this attitude. Only then can you get back on your feet and start afresh.

"Rock 'n' Roll" does not mean just enjoying life. It means to demolish the mistaken values of society. I ask you, the people of the "Rock 'n' Roll" generation: Awaken and rise. Knock some sense into the young people and encourage them to work harder. There was once a time when the students protested at various universities. Please recall that kind of energy and tell others, "Now is the time to fight a revolution for the sake of God. Rise, everyone. What are you waiting for? Don't be lazy. Don't just be sleeping at home. Don't live off your parents without working. Don't just expect a pay raise. Don't depend on the government to raise wages for you or hand out subsidies. Instead, work properly and fight!" This is what I want to say.

Choose a life of service to the world

Many people [around this region] are probably fatigued from the prolonged aftermath of the earthquake, so of course, kind words and various subsidies and services may be helpful. However, we must also do what we can ourselves. We should have a strong will to create a better future, enrich our lives every single day, and fulfill what we ought to do.

Ask yourself,

"What can I do today? What can I do tomorrow?"

This is a battle with yourself.

You will eventually leave this world

Before you are 100, 110, or 120 years old.

But do not worry about

What will happen to you after that.

Just believe in me.

Do not let your mind waver anymore.

Make the most of your day every day

And do what you must do to the end.

This is extremely important.

Choosing the Light means

Choosing a life of service to the world.

This is for your own good, as well.

It is definitely wrong to believe that

Life ends with death.

Your real life starts after you die.

Life in this world is a training period for that.

So you must keep fighting in this world

Through hardships and difficulties

And despite the suffering you may have,
Take on the challenge to give love to others.

Defeat the coronavirus with El Cantare belief!
This is my message [*audience applauds*].
The world will continue
Sinking into darkness for a while,
But please fill your region with
Amazingly energetic and cheerful people.
It is important to never let go of your hopes.

Do what you can.
Have hope.
God will bestow trials on human beings
Because He feels the need to "clean" the Earth
And "purify" humankind,
But there is more to it.
After wiping out all the wrongs,
God will try to give rise to something new and right.
Please believe in this.
Let us live out our lives to the fullest
And give it our all.

EDITOR'S NOTES

1 Refer to *Spiritual Reading of Novel Coronavirus Infection Originated in China* [Tokyo: HS Press, 2020].

2 As of June 2024, there are over 100,000 members in Nepal.

3 Before this lecture, a video was shown to announce that a Happy Science movie was awarded at an International Film Festival.

For a deeper understanding of
The Earth says: "All you need is Love"
see other books below by Ryuho Okawa:

The Laws of Faith [New York: IRH Press, 2018]

The Road to Cultivate Yourself [New York: IRH Press, 2023]

Spiritual Reading of Novel Coronavirus Infection Originated in China [Tokyo: HS Press, 2020]

ABOUT THE AUTHOR

Founder and CEO of Happy Science Group.

Ryuho Okawa was born on July 7th 1956, in Tokushima, Japan. After graduating from the University of Tokyo with a law degree, he joined a Tokyo-based trading house. While working at its New York headquarters, he studied international finance at the Graduate Center of the City University of New York. In 1981, he attained Great Enlightenment and became aware that he is El Cantare with a mission to bring salvation to all humankind.

In 1986, he established Happy Science. It now has members in 171 countries across the world, with more than 700 branches and temples as well as 10,000 missionary houses around the world.

He has given over 3,500 lectures (of which more than 150 are in English) and published over 3,150 books (of which more than 600 are Spiritual Interview Series), many of which are translated into 42 languages. Along with *The Laws of the Sun* and *The Laws of Hell*, many of the books have become best sellers or million sellers. To date, Happy Science has produced 27 movies under his supervision. He has given the original story and concept and is also the Executive Producer. He has also composed music and written lyrics for over 450 pieces.

Moreover, he is the Founder of Happy Science University and Happy Science Academy (Junior and Senior High School), Founder and President of the Happiness Realization Party, Founder and Honorary Headmaster of Happy Science Institute of Government and Management, Founder of IRH Press Co., Ltd., and the Chairperson of NEW STAR PRODUCTION Co., Ltd. and ARI Production Co., Ltd.

WHO IS EL CANTARE?

El Cantare means "the Light of the Earth." He is the Supreme God of the Earth who has been guiding humankind since the beginning of Genesis, and He is the Creator of the universe. He is whom Jesus called Father and Muhammad called Allah and is *Ame-no-Mioya-Gami*, Japanese Father God. Different parts of El Cantare's core consciousness have descended to Earth in the past, once as Alpha and another as Elohim. His branch spirits, such as Shakyamuni Buddha and Hermes, have descended to Earth many times and helped to flourish many civilizations. To unite various religions and to integrate various fields of study in order to build a new civilization on Earth, a part of the core consciousness has descended to Earth as Master Ryuho Okawa.

Alpha is a part of the core consciousness of El Cantare who descended to Earth around 330 million years ago. Alpha preached Earth's Truths to harmonize and unify Earth-born humans and space people who came from other planets.

Elohim is a part of the core consciousness of El Cantare who descended to Earth around 150 million years ago. He gave wisdom, mainly on the differences between light and darkness, good and evil.

Ame-no-Mioya-Gami (Japanese Father God) is the Creator God and the Father God who appears in ancient literature, *Hotsuma Tsutae*. It is believed that He descended on the foothills of Mt. Fuji about 30,000 years ago and built the Fuji dynasty, which is the root of the Japanese civilization. With justice as the central pillar, Ame-no-Mioya-Gami's teachings spread to ancient civilizations of other countries in the world.

Shakyamuni Buddha was born as a prince into the Shakya clan in India around 2,600 years ago. When he was 29 years old, he renounced the world and sought enlightenment. He later attained Great Enlightenment and founded Buddhism.

Hermes is one of the 12 Olympian gods in Greek mythology, but the spiritual Truth is that he taught the teachings of love and progress around 4,300 years ago which became the origin of the current Western civilization. He is a hero who truly existed.

Ophealis was born in Greece around 6,500 years ago and was the leader who took an expedition to as far as Egypt. He is the God of miracles, prosperity, and arts, and is known as Osiris in Egyptian mythology.

Rient Arl Croud was born as a king of the ancient Incan Empire around 7,000 years ago and taught about the mysteries of the mind. In the heavenly world, he is responsible for the interactions that take place between various planets.

Thoth was an almighty leader who built the golden age of the Atlantic civilization around 12,000 years ago. In Egyptian mythology, he is known as God Thoth.

Ra Mu was a leader who built the golden age of the civilization of Mu around 17,000 years ago. As a religious leader and a politician, he ruled by uniting religion and politics.

ABOUT HAPPY SCIENCE

Happy Science is a religious group founded on the faith in El Cantare who is the God of the Earth, and the Creator of the universe. The essence of human beings is the soul that was created by God, and we all are children of God. God is our true parent, so in our souls, we have a fundamental desire to "believe in God, love God, and get closer to God." And, we can get closer to God by living with God's Will as our own. In Happy Science, we call this the "Exploration of Right Mind." More specifically, it means to practice the Fourfold Path, which consists of "Love, Wisdom, Self-Reflection, and Progress."

Love: Love means "love that gives," or mercy. God hopes for the happiness of all people. Therefore, living with God's Will as our own means to start by practicing "love that gives."

Wisdom: God's love is boundless. It is important to learn various Truths in order to understand the heart of God.

Self-Reflection: Once you learn the heart of God and the difference between His mind and yours, you should strive to bring your own mind closer to the mind of God—that process is called self-reflection. Self-reflection also includes meditation and prayer.

Progress: Since God hopes for the happiness of all people, you should also make progress in your love, and make an effort to realize utopia in which everyone in your society, country, and eventually all humankind can become happy.

As we practice this Fourfold Path, our souls will advance toward God step by step. That is when we can attain real happiness—our souls' desire to get closer to God comes true.

In Happy Science, we conduct activities to make ourselves happy through belief in Lord El Cantare and to spread this faith to the world and bring happiness to all. We welcome you to join our activities!

We hold events and activities to help you practice the Fourfold Path at our branches, temples, missionary centers, and missionary houses

Love: We hold various volunteering activities. Our members conduct missionary work together as the greatest practice of love.

Wisdom: We offer our comprehensive collection of books of Truth, many of which are available online and at Happy Science locations. In addition, we offer numerous opportunities such as seminars or book clubs to learn the Truth.

Self-Reflection: We offer opportunities to polish your mind through self-reflection, meditation, and prayer. Many members have experienced improvement in their human relationships by changing their own minds.

Progress: We also offer seminars to enhance your power of influence. Because it is also important to do well at work to make society better, we hold seminars to improve your work and management skills.

BOOKS BY RYUHO OKAWA

The Laws of the Sun, the first publication of the Laws Series, ranked in the annual best-selling list in Japan in 1994. Since then, the Laws Series' titles have ranked in the annual best-selling list every year for more than three decades, setting socio-cultural trends in Japan and around the world. The first three Laws Series are *The Laws of the Sun*, *The Golden Laws*, and *The Laws of Eternity*.

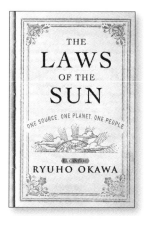

The Laws of the Sun

One Source, One Planet, One People

Paperback • 288 pages • $15.95
ISBN: 978-1-942125-43-3 (Oct. 25, 2018)

IMAGINE IF YOU COULD ASK GOD why He created this world and about the spiritual laws He used to shape us and everything around us. If we could understand His designs and intentions, we could discover what our goals in life should be and whether our actions move us closer to those goals or farther away.

At a young age, a spiritual calling prompted Ryuho Okawa to outline what he innately understood to be universal truths for all humankind. In *The Laws of the Sun*, Okawa outlines these laws of the universe and provides a road map for living one's life with greater purpose and meaning. In this powerful book, Ryuho Okawa reveals the transcendent nature of consciousness and the secrets of the multidimensional universe as well as the meaning of humans that exist within it. By understanding the different stages of love and following the Buddhist Eightfold Path, he believes we can speed up our eternal process of development. *The Laws of the Sun* shows the way to realize true happiness—a happiness that continues from this world through the other.

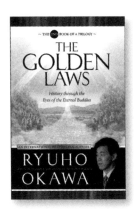

The Golden Laws

History through the Eyes of
the Eternal Buddha

E-book • 204 pages • $13.99
ISBN: 978-1-941779-82-8 (Sep. 24, 2015)

Throughout history, Great Guiding Spirits have been present on Earth in both the East and the West at crucial points in human history to further our spiritual development. *The Golden Laws* reveals how the Divine Plan has been unfolding on Earth, and outlines 5,000 years of the secret history of humankind. Once we understand the true course of history, through past, present, and into the future, we cannot help but become aware of the significance of our spiritual mission in the present age.

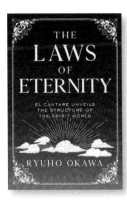

The Laws of Eternity

El Cantare Unveils the Structure of
the Spirit World

Paperback • 200 pages • $17.95
ISBN: 978-1-958655-16-0 (May 15, 2024)

"Where do we come from and where do we go after death?" This unparalleled book offers us complete answers to life's most important questions that we all are confronted with at some point or another. This book reveals the eternal mysteries and the ultimate secrets of Earth's Spirit Group that have been covered by the veil of legends and myths. Encountering the long-hidden Eternal Truths that are revealed for the first time in human history will change the way you live your life now.

The Eternal Buddha

Now, Here, Is the Imperishable Light

Hardcover • 180 pages • $17.95
ISBN: 978-1-958655-19-1 (Sep 15, 2024)

This book is a powerful source of guidance for those seeking Truth.

Embedded within, you will find the infinite wisdom of Eternal Buddha and come to realize that you are not just a physical being, but an eternal soul of brilliant light.

This book will help you discover the true origin of your soul, why you have chosen to be born in this time, and why having faith is important.

Through the words of Eternal Buddha, unlock the boundless treasures of enlightenment given to humankind in this modern era.

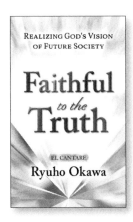

Faithful to the Truth

Realizing God's Vision of Future Society

Paperback • 164 pages • $20.00
ISBN: 979-8-887371-12-2 (Apr. 24, 2024)

The spiritual truth and the forecasts written in this book are messages from God that people worldwide should know right now. The world is on the verge of collapse. So, now is the time for people to listen to what Okawa is saying, as he is the one who knows the Truth, who can see God's vision, and who is trying to guide humanity in the right direction.

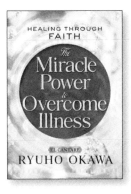

The Miracle Power to Overcome Illness

Healing Through Faith

Paperback • 256 pages • $17.95
ISBN: 978-1-958655-17-7 (Jul 15, 2024)

With his deep spiritual insight, Okawa points out the spiritual causes of mental and physical problems and the ways to overcome them. Transcend your worldly understanding of illness, awaken to the power of faith, and make efforts to improve yourself, step by step. Then, surely, you will receive the miracle power from the heavenly world.

Recommended Books

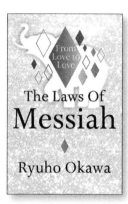

The Laws Of Messiah

From Love to Love

Paperback • 248 pages • $16.95
ISBN: 978-1-942125-90-7 (Jan. 31, 2022)

"What is Messiah?" This book carries an important message of love and guidance to people living now from the Modern-Day Messiah or the Modern-Day Savior. It also reveals the secret of Shambhala, the spiritual center of Earth, as well as the truth that this spiritual center is currently in danger of perishing and what we can do to protect this sacred place. Discover the true love of God and the ideal practice of faith, here, in this book.

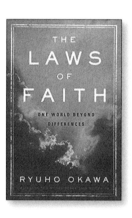

The Laws of Faith

One World Beyond Differences

Paperback • 208 pages • $15.95
ISBN: 978-1-942125-34-1 (Mar. 31, 2018)

In this book, Ryuho Okawa preaches the core teachings of the world religion and the faith in the God of Earth. By integrating logical and spiritual viewpoints, Okawa gives answers to modern-day problems that traditional religions cannot solve. Through this book, you will learn to go beyond different values, harmonize with each other and between nations, and create a world filled with peace and prosperity.

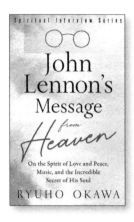

John Lennon's Message from Heaven

On the Spirit of Love and Peace, Music, and the Incredible Secret of His Soul

Paperback • 310 pages • $13.95
ISBN: 979-8887370026 (Apr. 11, 2020)

In this book, the spirit of John Lennon talks about the secret to his explosive popularity and what he wanted to tell others about the Establishment, the Vietnam War, the Black liberation movement and racial discrimination, and more. You will learn the inner essence of John Lennon and the heavenly aspect of rock music that helps people and the world.

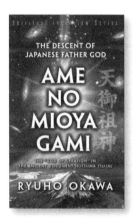

The Descent of Japanese Father God Ame-no-Mioya-Gami

The "God of Creation" in the Ancient Document *Hotsuma Tsutae*

Paperback • 276 pages • $14.95
ISBN: 978-1-943928-35-4 (Feb. 12, 2022)

By reading this book, you can find the origin of bushido (samurai spirit) and understand how the ancient Japanese civilization influenced other countries. Now that the world is in confusion, Japan is expected to awaken to its true origin and courageously rise to bring justice to the world.

The Ten Principles from El Cantare Volume I

Ryuho Okawa's First Lectures on His Basic Teachings

Paperback • 232 pages • $16.95
ISBN: 978-1-942125-85-3 (Dec. 15, 2021)

This book contains the historic lectures given on the first five principles of the Ten Principles of Happy Science from the author, Ryuho Okawa, who is revered as World Teacher. These lectures produced an enthusiastic fellowship in Happy Science Japan and became the foundation of the current global utopian movement. You can learn the essence of Okawa's teachings and the secret behind the rapid growth of the Happy Science movement in simple language.

The Ten Principles from El Cantare Volume II

Ryuho Okawa's First Lectures on His Wish to Save the World

Paperback • 272 pages • $16.95
ISBN: 978-1-942125-86-0 (May 3, 2022)

A sequel to *The Ten Principles from El Cantare Volume I*. Volume II reveals the Creator's three major inventions; the secret of the creation of human souls, the meaning of time, and 'happiness' as life's purpose. By reading this book, you can not only improve yourself but learn how to make difference in society and create an ideal, utopian world.

What Is Happy Science?

Best Selection of Ryuho Okawa's Early Lectures (Volume 1)

Paperback • 256 pages • $17.95
ISBN: 978-1-942125-99-0 (Aug. 25, 2023)

The Best Selection series is a collection of Ryuho Okawa's passionate lectures during the ages of 32 to 33 that revealed the mission and goal of Happy Science. This book contains the eternal Truth, including the meaning of life, the secret of the mind, the true meaning of love, the mystery of the universe, and how to end hatred and world conflicts.

The Laws of Happiness

Love, Wisdom, Self-Reflection and Progress

Paperback • 264 pages • $16.95
ISBN: 978-1-942125-70-9 (Aug. 28, 2020)

Happiness is not found outside us; it is found within us. It is in how we think, how we look at our lives, and how we devote our hearts to the work we do. Discover how the Fourfold Path of Love, Wisdom, Self-Reflection, and Progress create a life of sustainable happiness.

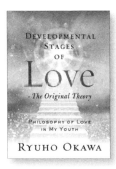

Developmental Stages of Love - The Original Theory

Philosophy of Love in My Youth

Hardcover • 200 pages • $17.95
ISBN: 978-1-942125-94-5 (Jun. 15, 2022)

This book is about author Ryuho Okawa's original philosophy of love which serves as the foundation of love in chapter three of *The Laws of the Sun*. It consists of a series of short essays authored during the age of 25 through 28 while he was working as a young promising business elite at an international trading company after attaining the Great Enlightenment in 1981. This is an excellent book to contemplate the true meaning of love in our everyday life.

The Essence of Buddha

The Path to Enlightenment

Paperback • 208 pages • $14.95
ISBN: 978-1-942125-06-8 (Oct.1, 2016)

In this book, Ryuho Okawa imparts in simple and accessible language his wisdom about the essence of Shakyamuni Buddha's philosophy of life and enlightenment—teachings that have been inspiring people all over the world for over 2,500 years. By offering a new perspective on core Buddhist thoughts that have long been cloaked in mystique, Okawa brings these teachings to life for modern people. *The Essence of Buddha* distills a way of life that anyone can practice to achieve a life of self-growth, compassionate living, and true happiness.

The True Eightfold Path

Guideposts for Self-Innovation

Paperback • 256 pages • $16.95
ISBN: 978-1-942125-80-8 (Mar. 30, 2021)

This book explains how we can apply the Eightfold Path, one of the main pillars of Shakyamuni Buddha's teachings, as everyday guideposts in the modern age to achieve self-innovation to live better and make positive changes in these uncertain times.

The Rebirth of Buddha

My Eternal Disciples, Hear My Words

Paperback • 280 pages • $17.95
ISBN: 978-1-942125-95-2 (Jul. 15, 2022)

These are the messages of Buddha who has returned to this modern age as promised to his eternal beloved disciples. They are in simple words and poetic style, yet contain profound messages. Once you start reading these passages, you will remember why you chose to be born in the same era as Buddha. Listen to the voices of your Eternal Master and awaken to your calling.

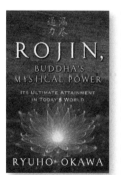

Rojin, Buddha's Mystical Power

Its Ultimate Attainment in Today's World

Paperback • 224 pages • $16.95
ISBN: 978-1-942125-82-2 (Sep. 24, 2021)

In this book, Ryuho Okawa has redefined the traditional Buddhist term *Rojin* to fit modern society as follows: The ability for individuals with great spiritual powers to live in the world as people with common sense while using their abilities to the optimal level. This book will unravel the mystery of the mind and lead you to the path to enlightenment.

Words of Wisdom Series

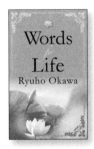

Words for Life

Paperback • 136 pages • $15.95
ISBN: 979-8-88737-089-7 (Mar. 16, 2023)

Ryuho Okawa has written over 3,150 books on various topics. To help readers find the teachings that are beneficial for them out of the extensive teachings, the author has written 100 phrases and put them together. Inside you will find words of wisdom that will help you improve your mindset and lead you to live a meaningful and happy life.

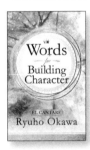

Words for Building Character

Paperback • 140 pages • $15.95
ISBN: 979-8-88737-091-0 (Jun. 21, 2023)

When your life comes to an end, what you can bring with you to the other world is your enlightenment, in other words, the character that you build in this lifetime. If you can read, relish, and truly understand the meaning of these religious phrases, you will be able to attain happiness that transcends this world and the next.

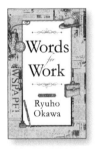

Words for Work

Paperback • 140 pages • $15.95
ISBN: 979-8-88737-090-3 (Jul. 20, 2023)

Through his personal experiences at work, Ryuho Okawa has created these phrases regarding philosophies and practical wisdom about work. This book will be of great use to you throughout your career. Every day you can contemplate and gain tips on how to better your work as well as deepen your insight into company management.

Words to Read in Times of Illness

Hardcover • 136 pages • $17.95
ISBN: 978-1-958655-07-8 (Sep. 15, 2023)

Ryuho Okawa has written 100 Healing Messages to comfort the souls of those going through any illness. When we are ill, it is an ideal time for us to contemplate recent and past events, as well as our relationship with the people around us. It is a chance for us to take inventory of our emotions and thoughts.

MUSIC BY RYUHO OKAWA

El Cantare Ryuho Okawa Original Songs

A song celebrating Lord God / With Savior

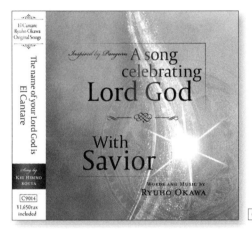

Words & Music by Ryuho Okawa

1. A song celebrating Lord God—Renewal ver.
2. With Savior—Renewal ver.
3. A song celebrating Lord God—Renewal ver. (Instrumental)
4. With Savior—Renewal ver. (Instrumental)
5. With Savior—Renewal ver. (Instrumental with chorus)

"The True Words Spoken By Buddha"

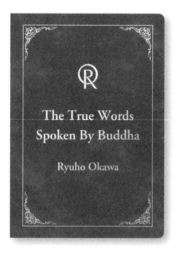

"The True Words Spoken By Buddha" is an English sutra given directly from the spirit of Shakyamuni Buddha, who is a part of Master Ryuho Okawa's subconscious. The words in this sutra are not of a mere human being but are the words of God or Buddha sent directly from the ninth dimension, which is the highest realm of the Earth's Spirit World.

"The True Words Spoken By Buddha" is an essential sutra for us to connect and live with God or Buddha's Will as our own.

MEMBERSHIPS

MEMBERSHIP

If you would like to know more about Happy Science, please consider becoming a member. Those who pledge to believe in Lord El Cantare and wish to learn more can join us.

When you become a member, you will receive the following sutras: "The True Words Spoken By Buddha," "Prayer to the Lord" and "Prayer to Guardian and Guiding Spirits."

DEVOTEE MEMBER

If you would like to learn the teachings of Happy Science and walk the path of faith, become a Devotee member who pledges devotion to the Three Treasures, which are Buddha, Dharma, and Sangha. Buddha refers to Lord El Cantare, Master Ryuho Okawa. Dharma refers to Master Ryuho Okawa's teachings. Sangha refers to Happy Science. Devoting to the Three Treasures will let your Buddha nature shine, and you will enter the path to attain true freedom of the mind.

Becoming a devotee means you become Buddha's disciple. You will discipline your mind and act to bring happiness to society.

✉ EMAIL or ☎ PHONE CALL
Please turn to the contact information page.

☎ ONLINE ⎡member.happy-science.org/signup/ ◉⎤

CONTACT INFORMATION

Happy Science is a worldwide organization with branches and temples around the globe. For full details, visit happy-science.org. The following are some of our main Happy Science locations:

UNITED STATES AND CANADA

New York
79 Franklin St., New York, NY 10013, USA
Phone: 1-212-343-7972
Fax: 1-212-343-7973
Email: ny@happy-science.org
Website: happyscience-usa.org

New Jersey
66 Hudson St., #2R, Hoboken, NJ 07030, USA
Phone: 1-201-313-0127
Email: nj@happy-science.org
Website: happyscience-usa.org

Chicago
2300 Barrington Rd., Suite #400,
Hoffman Estates, IL 60169, USA
Phone: 1-630-937-3077
Email: chicago@happy-science.org
Website: happyscience-usa.org

Florida
5208 8th St., Zephyrhills, FL 33542, USA
Phone: 1-813-715-0000
Fax: 1-813-715-0010
Email: florida@happy-science.org
Website: happyscience-usa.org

Atlanta
1874 Piedmont Ave., NE Suite 360-C
Atlanta, GA 30324, USA
Phone: 1-404-892-7770
Email: atlanta@happy-science.org
Website: happyscience-usa.org

San Francisco
525 Clinton St.
Redwood City, CA 94062, USA
Phone & Fax: 1-650-363-2777
Email: sf@happy-science.org
Website: happyscience-usa.org

Los Angeles
1590 E. Del Mar Blvd., Pasadena,
CA 91106, USA
Phone: 1-626-395-7775
Fax: 1-626-395-7776
Email: la@happy-science.org
Website: happyscience-usa.org

Orange County
16541 Gothard St. Suite 104
Huntington Beach, CA 92647
Phone: 1-714-659-1501
Email: oc@happy-science.org
Website: happyscience-usa.org

San Diego
7841 Balboa Ave. Suite #202
San Diego, CA 92111, USA
Phone: 1-626-395-7775
Fax: 1-626-395-7776
E-mail: sandiego@happy-science.org
Website: happyscience-usa.org

Hawaii
Phone: 1-808-591-9772
Fax: 1-808-591-9776
Email: hi@happy-science.org
Website: happyscience-usa.org

Kauai
3343 Kanakolu Street, Suite 5
Lihue, HI 96766, USA
Phone: 1-808-822-7007
Fax: 1-808-822-6007
Email: kauai-hi@happy-science.org
Website: happyscience-usa.org

Toronto
845 The Queensway
Etobicoke, ON M8Z 1N6, Canada
Phone: 1-416-901-3747
Email: toronto@happy-science.org
Website: happy-science.ca

Vancouver
#201-2607 East 49th Avenue,
Vancouver, BC, V5S 1J9, Canada
Phone: 1-604-437-7735
Fax: 1-604-437-7764
Email: vancouver@happy-science.org
Website: happy-science.ca

INTERNATIONAL

Tokyo
1-6-7 Togoshi, Shinagawa,
Tokyo, 142-0041, Japan
Phone: 81-3-6384-5770
Fax: 81-3-6384-5776
Email: tokyo@happy-science.org
Website: happy-science.org

London
3 Margaret St.
London, W1W 8RE United Kingdom
Phone: 44-20-7323-9255
Fax: 44-20-7323-9344
Email: eu@happy-science.org
Website: www.happyscience-uk.org

Sydney
516 Pacific Highway, Lane Cove North,
2066 NSW, Australia
Phone: 61-2-9411-2877
Fax: 61-2-9411-2822
Email: sydney@happy-science.org

Sao Paulo
Rua. Domingos de Morais 1154,
Vila Mariana, Sao Paulo SP
CEP 04010-100, Brazil
Phone: 55-11-5088-3800
Email: sp@happy-science.org
Website: happyscience.com.br

Jundiai
Rua Congo, 447, Jd. Bonfiglioli
Jundiai-CEP, 13207-340, Brazil
Phone: 55-11-4587-5952
Email: jundiai@happy-science.org

Seoul
74, Sadang-ro 27-gil,
Dongjak-gu, Seoul, Korea
Phone: 82-2-3478-8777
Fax: 82-2-3478-9777
Email: korea@happy-science.org

Taipei
No. 89, Lane 155, Dunhua N. Road,
Songshan District, Taipei City 105, Taiwan
Phone: 886-2-2719-9377
Fax: 886-2-2719-5570
Email: taiwan@happy-science.org

Taichung
No. 146, Minzu Rd., Central Dist.,
Taichung City 400001, Taiwan
Phone: 886-4-22233777
Email: taichung@happy-science.org

Kuala Lumpur
No 22A, Block 2, Jalil Link Jalan Jalil Jaya
2, Bukit Jalil 57000,
Kuala Lumpur, Malaysia
Phone: 60-3-8998-7877
Fax: 60-3-8998-7977
Email: malaysia@happy-science.org
Website: happyscience.org.my

Kathmandu
Kathmandu Metropolitan City,
Ward No. 15, Ring Road, Kimdol,
Sitapaila Kathmandu, Nepal
Phone: 977-1-537-2931
Email: nepal@happy-science.org

Kampala
Plot 877 Rubaga Road, Kampala
P.O. Box 34130 Kampala, Uganda
Email: uganda@happy-science.org

ABOUT HS PRESS

HS Press is an imprint of IRH Press Co., Ltd. IRH Press Co., Ltd., based in Tokyo, was founded in 1987 as a publishing division of Happy Science. IRH Press publishes religious and spiritual books, journals, and magazines and also operates broadcast and film production enterprises. For more information, visit *okawabooks.com*.

Follow us on:

f Facebook: Okawa Books   **◯** Instagram: OkawaBooks
▶ Youtube: Okawa Books   **🐦** Twitter: Okawa Books
𝓟 Pinterest: Okawa Books   **g** Goodreads: Ryuho Okawa

——— **NEWSLETTER** ———

To receive book-related news, promotions, and events, please subscribe to our newsletter below.

⟲ okawabooks.com/pages/subscribe

——— **AUDIO / VISUAL MEDIA** ———

YOUTUBE

PODCAST

Introduction of Ryuho Okawa's titles; topics ranging from self-help, current affairs, spirituality, religion, and the universe.